Finding My Way

Out of the darkness, into the light

Siobhán Kangataran

Copyright © 2018 Siobhán Kangataran

All rights reserved.

ISBN: 9781980482284

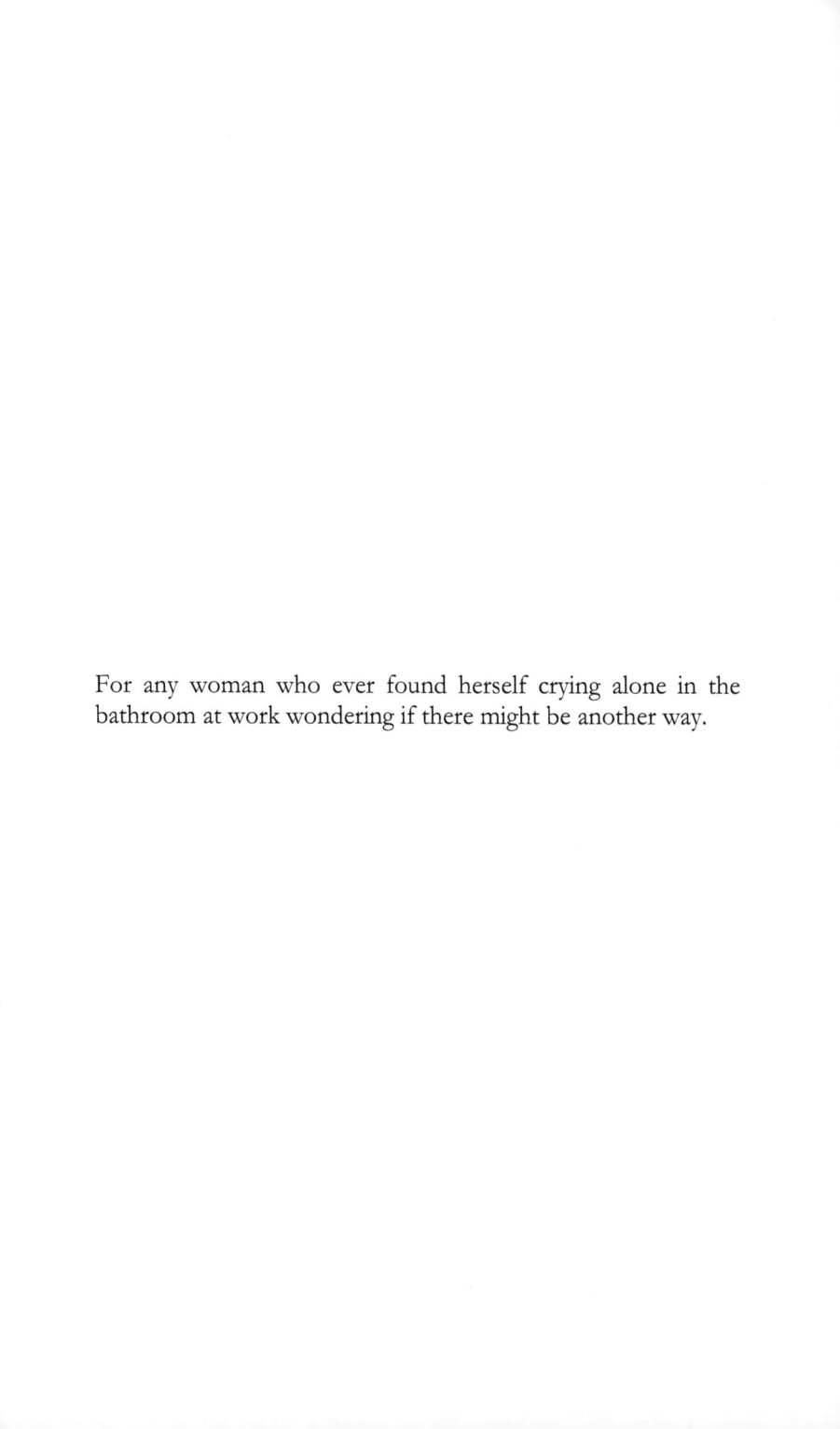

For any woman who ever found herself crying alone in the bathroom at work wondering if there might be another way.

"Owning our story can be hard but not nearly as difficult as spending our lives running from it. Embracing our vulnerabilities is risky but not nearly as dangerous as giving up on love and belonging and joy—the experiences that make us the most vulnerable. Only when we are brave enough to explore the darkness will we discover the infinite power of our light."

- Brené Brown

CONTENTS

	How to Read This Book	ix
	Introduction	xi
1	Pit of Darkness	1
2	Clawing My Way Out	9
3	Addicted to Inspiration	13
4	Finding My Voice	17
5	Cultivating Joy	21
6	Calm Before the Storm	27
7	Crying Over Spilt Coffee	31
8	Breakthrough (or Breakdown)	37
9	Magical Moment	43
10	Finding My Tribe	49
11	(Reluctantly) Embracing Creativity	55
12	Absolute Clarity	61
13	Enough is Enough is Enough	67
14	Escaping the City	75
15	Taking Small Steps	83
16	Blossoming at Blooms	89

17	To Coach or Not to Coach	93
18	Letting Go	99
19	Darkest Before the Dawn	103
	Final Thoughts	111
	Resources	115
	Acknowledgements	119
	About the Author	121

HOW TO READ THIS BOOK

I wrote this book to share my learning – to share my journey from the darkness of fear and anxiety into the light of creativity and inspiration over the course of an extremely challenging period of my life. So it's intended to be read in chronological order, but perhaps not necessarily all at once.

It's taken me years to understand and process what I've learned, so I wouldn't expect it to be easy for my story to make sense or sink in very quickly to anyone else, although I hope that reading my story helps you make a little more sense of your own journey.

I would like to invite you to use this book as an opportunity for reflection – at regular intervals I will share the lessons I learned along my journey, and I will invite you to reflect and ask yourself what I hope will be useful and thought-provoking questions. If it feels appropriate, I invite you to share your learning with us in the safe space of the ToGetHer Further Facebook group (www.facebook.com/groups/getherfurther).

I will also share some useful resources – you'll find them scattered throughout the book, or you can access them all at http://bit.ly/FindingMyWayResources. They're not always the resources I used myself at each stage of my journey, but the ones that I wish I'd known about then. Essentially, I'm sharing the gift of my hindsight, in the hope that it helps you get to where you're going that little bit quicker.

As you read this book you may find some elements more uncomfortable or challenging for you – feel free to take your time, stop and reflect when you need, or read my story all the way through and return to the more reflective elements later.

Know that I am with you; know that you are not alone.

Siobhán Kangataran

INTRODUCTION

I thought I was happy. Or at least, I was successful, which is the same as happy, right? But then why did everything feel wrong? Why did I feel like I was struggling to keep my head above water? Why did I feel so terrified so much of the time?

I was earning more money than I ever had before, working on a prestigious project, in a position of great responsibility. I was in a loving, respectful relationship with an incredibly understanding, supportive boyfriend, and we lived in a spacious flat we were renting together in London, while saving to buy a house in the countryside.

I should have felt grateful for all of these amazing opportunities and gifts I had in my life. But instead I felt trapped at work. Terrified. Like a caged animal. As if there was no way out. I just needed to keep my head down and work my way through the darkness, and surely light would come to me from somewhere. Surely someone or something would save me from myself?

Or maybe, I was going to have to save myself.

Claw my way out from the darkness and into the light.

This is my story.

1 PIT OF DARKNESS

I knew something was wrong when I didn't want to go to work anymore. Not just the usual Monday morning blues, but full on toddler-style tantrums bubbling up in me at the thought of walking into the office. I had been trying to avoid dealing with the reality of my intense new job – I'd been distracting myself with positive, uplifting playlists that I would blast myself with on my all-too-short bus route to work. As the last few stops appeared, I would feel this sinking sense of dread in the pit of my stomach. I couldn't avoid it any longer – I was going to have to face the terrifying reality before me.

It was August 2015, and I was 4 months in to a challenging new project management role on a prestigious property development in London. I had recently changed industries from public sector railway construction to private sector luxury properties, and my perfectionist self was seriously struggling with taking on the challenge. I was paralysed by Impostor Syndrome, terrified that someone was going to come along at any moment to tap me on the shoulder and say, "We've realised you have no idea what you're doing, and we'd like you to leave..." Every day that that didn't happen felt like a relief, as if I'd dodged a bullet.

I kept trying to make my commute more and more pleasant, i.e., by distracting myself more. My incredibly supportive boyfriend began driving me to the office on his own way to work, which made the first 20 minutes so pleasant – I could almost forget where we were going, and pretend he was taking me somewhere that didn't terrify me so much, somewhere fun and easy and exciting. But then we would get to the point where he had to turn towards my office, and the dread would kick in, harder than ever before. Pulling up outside the entrance, the emotions would bubble up in me, as I'd try to be brave, try to be the professional, competent adult I needed to be in order to get through the day. I would paste a smile on my face, and stride in the door, hoping today would be different, that today would be the day I would finally understand what the hell I was doing there.

Eventually, I got to a point where I was getting bored of my own suffering. I could see my poor boyfriend had no idea how to help me, and although I had tried asking for help in the office, I felt as though things were too dark for me to make them understand what I needed. I was fortunate that I was already seeing a therapist, and she was a weekly source of relief from the chaos of my existence, but I needed to do something different if I was going to change my painful daily routine.

I wanted to quit my job, so badly, but the perfectionist in me was terrified of admitting failure. I had been advised by friends and former colleagues to "give it six months", to "wait and see, it will get easier", so giving up less than five months into the challenge felt like a public statement of weakness. I'd come this far, surely it would indeed get easier if I could just give it time. But how was I going to make it another six weeks when I didn't even want to face another day?

I decided to sit and reflect on the previous few months, and how increasingly difficult they'd been, and I realised that not all of the days had been bad. Some had been better than others – usually it was the days where I had managed to get out of bed a little earlier to sit and use my Headspace app. This felt like an amazing insight, a realization that there might be something I could do to change how I felt about work, that I didn't have to suffer as if someone was forcing something unbearable on me.

I knew I needed to change something about my commute – that I had to stop avoiding the fact that I was indeed going to work, stop trying to pretend an alternate reality existed, and actually face what lay before me.

So I decided to try a new morning routine to set myself up for a good day. Starting 1st September 2015, for 30 days, I would get up at 6am, do five Sun Salutations (yoga flow sequences), 10 minutes of Headspace, and let myself free-write in my journal – anything to create some space to help me start the day a little calmer, more grounded, and less terrified. The whole routine took just over 30 minutes, so it wasn't a huge imposition, but the biggest difference was that I gave myself permission to arrive at the office half an hour later than the 7.45am start I'd previously set myself. I decided that starting my day at 8.15am, calmly and clearly, was a far wiser investment of time for both me and my project, regardless of any 'facetime' credits I lost in the process.

I also made the decision to walk to work every day, whatever the weather, for those 30 days, in an effort to face my fearful commute head on. To stop avoiding the inevitable, to stop acting like a victim, and to step up to empower myself to make the most of this time in my day, rather than trying to numb myself as I wished my life away. The walk took around the same amount of time as my bus route, but with every single step, I was mentally and physically choosing to go to work, and as I got closer to the office, rather than feeling dread and despair, I felt relief, because I could at least stop walking.

And finally, to make sure I was fully using my time to benefit myself, I decided to use my walk to listen to all those Ted Talks and podcasts people had been recommending to me over the years, but somehow I'd never found the time to listen. I started with Sheryl Sandberg, of course, listening to her Ted Talk on Why We Have Too Few Women Leaders, and by the time I got to work I was practically skipping. I wasn't the only woman struggling out there – there were plenty of us suffering in silence in various forms. But hearing this inspiring story reminded me that the suffering didn't have to be permanent, that there was a brighter future out there and if I could just hold on and stay focused, and stick to my new, healthier plans - I would eventually get there.

I stuck to my 30 day routine religiously – helped by the support of my boyfriend on the days where I would hit 'snooze' on my alarm, he would rip back the duvet and literally kick me out of bed saying "I don't want a cranky girlfriend! Go do your Headspace!"

It hadn't taken long for me to feel the benefits of carving this time out for myself in the mornings – I was still very much struggling at work, but now I had a little more capacity to deal with things, and I was feeling my pain, rather than cutting myself off from it and trying to avoid what was happening. But these benefits clearly weren't just limited to the workplace – my boyfriend was seeing a much calmer girlfriend returning home in the evenings, one who was a little lighter, a lot less moody and exhausted, and even a little happier at times.

Little by little, I felt less scared, but more emotional – tears coming to my eyes more easily – less anxious, but more overwhelmed, realizing the enormity of the tasks I'd set for myself, both professionally and personally. One day at work I stood up to go to the bathroom to make myself cry, in an attempt to let some of this emotion out and make some space for myself to feel more in control. I realised this wasn't healthy, and clearly not sustainable.

Again I made time to reflect, and tried to think of times when I'd felt more optimistic about my role, or less alone in what I was going through. I remembered my friend Emily's 'Women in Media' networking group – it had felt amazing to meet women from other walks of life and hear what challenges they were going through, for me to realise I wasn't the only one who was struggling. I messaged her immediately to see when the next event would be held, but there wasn't one arranged anytime soon. So I thought that maybe I should look into 'Women in Project Management', to find other women in similar roles or positions as me, that maybe they would understand what I was going through even better.

I googled 'Women in Project Management', and as luck (or fate?) would have it there was an annual conference coming up in two weeks, run by the Association for Project Management's women's group. I booked my place immediately, and told my (male) colleagues I was taking the day off to attend the event. They were dismissive when I told them what I was attending, telling me that it was "sexist" to aim events at women, and asking "what about the men in project management?"

I was nervous about being so open with them, being so vulnerable and visible, but I somehow managed to confidently say that it was important for me to go, and that I knew I would get a lot from being there. Somehow I knew that women-only spaces were important to me, and that I needed to find myself some kindred spirits, if I was to truly find a way through my suffering.

Lessons I learned from this experience:

- Staying in this victim mode, waiting for someone else to rescue me, meant I was barely surviving, rather than thriving.
- My perfectionism was paralysing me from making any significant changes to my life, and I've since learned that perfectionism is not 'doing your best', it's fearing not being 'good enough', and doing everything you can to avoid it.
- I was the only one who could save me from myself.
- I couldn't keep avoiding my struggles – I had to face my challenges head on.
- I only began to find solutions when I took the time to reflect on what had helped me to feel better in the past.
- Making small, manageable changes allowed me to feel a noticeable difference quickly – I felt empowered by my own ability to take ownership of my situation.

Reflection questions for you:

- What helps you to feel more optimistic, motivated or inspired? When did you last make time to do this?
- Is there anything you're struggling with at the moment that you might be avoiding dealing with?
- When do you make time for yourself to reflect and observe your habits?
- What small changes could you make to your routine today to help you to stay connected to yourself?

Some useful resources for you:

- Read this blog post I wrote on why Self-Care is Not Selfish - *https://togetherfurther.org/2017/11/16/putting-your-own-lifejacket-on-first/*
- Read this article by Kate McCombs on Self-Care Strategies - *https://www.continuumcollective.org/blog/2017/3/7/5-self-care-strategies-that-arent-fucking-mani-pedis* (Warning: strong language)
- Try swapping your usual glossy mag for Psychologies Magazine *https://www.psychologies.co.uk/*
- Try Headspace or other meditation or mindfulness apps - *http://www.headspace.com/*
- Try Yoga With Adriene for free yoga videos via YouTube - *http://yogawithadriene.com/*
- Read The Gifts of Imperfection by Brené Brown
- Watch Brené Brown's Ted Talk on Listening to Shame
- Watch Sheryl Sandberg's Ted Talk on Why We Have Too Few Women Leaders *https://www.ted.com/talks/sheryl_sandberg_why_we_have_too_few_women_leaders*
- Watch Reshma Saujani's Ted Talk on Teach Girls Bravery, Not Perfection *https://www.ted.com/talks/reshma_saujani_teach_girls_bravery_not_perfection*
- Watch Andy Puddicombe's Ted Talk All it Takes is 10 Mindful Minutes *https://www.ted.com/talks/andy_puddicombe_all_it_takes_is_10_mindful_minutes*
- Watch Scott Dinsmore's Ted Talk How to Find Work You Love *https://www.ted.com/talks/scott_dinsmore_how_to_find_work_you_love*

Siobhán Kangataran

2 CLAWING MY WAY OUT

I'd never seen so many women in one place before, let alone so many female project managers. I hated networking, so I tried to avoid making small talk at first, but I was so keen to connect with other women there, dying to find kindred spirits who were struggling like I was. It didn't take long for me to find women who identified with my challenges – I quickly met some women who were well aware of the difficulty of often being the only woman in a room full of men, afraid of being seen as weak or emotional, and were struggling to hold it all together. I felt relieved just knowing it was ok to feel this way, and then, as I took my seat in an extremely crowded function room full of women, I felt empowered just by being there. It was as if I was drawing strength from our numbers – I felt lifted and held just by the sheer energy in the room. It was the murmurings of something magical rising within me.

The keynote speaker was Harriet Minter, who was the founder of the Guardian's Women in Leadership column, and has since gone on to even bigger and better things (including the Badass Women's Hour radio show and podcast). That day, it felt as if she had been sent to speak directly to me, particularly when she encouraged us to draw on the lessons from Joseph Campbell's The Hero's Journey – to ask for help when we need it, rather than suffering in silence, trapped in our own pit of despair. Already I knew I was in the right place – simply by being in that room with so many women, listening to Harriet's inspiring words, I was finding my way towards clawing myself out of that pit.

The rest of the day passed by in a blur but, as inspiring as the whole day turned out to be, nothing landed quite as powerfully as Harriet's words at the beginning of the day. She had spoken in such a genuine, authentic, inspiring way – no bullshit, no gloss – just her being herself, sharing her story of how and why she had created the Women in Leadership section of the newspaper, and how it had become a runaway success ever since. She encouraged us to follow in her footsteps and Proceed Until Apprehended, essentially to ask for forgiveness rather than permission, if we are to make our dreams into a reality.

In so many ways, as my journey unfolded, it felt as if Harriet was always nearby, giving me the inspiration and motivation I needed, just when I needed it, from her original keynote speech, to watching her Ted Talks, and then following her weekly newsletter of the same name: Proceed Until Apprehended.

Looking back, I don't believe I had even dared to properly dream before I first heard Harriet speak, but I left the conference that day feeling as if I'd been given a mission to dream big, to achieve more with my life, safe in the knowledge that I was never going to feel alone again.

Lessons I learned from this experience:

- There is so much strength in numbers! It's so important for us to find others who share our reality.
- The power of authenticity - people's words carry so much more weight when they share the setbacks they experienced, rather than pretending to be perfect.
- The importance of asking for help - none of us can do this alone, we all need to let others help us every now and then.

Reflection questions for you:

- When did you last find yourself surrounded by likeminded people?
- When was the last time you found yourself inspired by someone's story?
- When did you last ask anyone for help with something you were struggling with?

Useful resources for you:

- Try using MeetUp to find people with similar interests to you
  https://www.meetup.com/
- Try Trigger Conversations to make real connections and have meaningful conversations
  https://www.triggerconversations.co.uk/
- Join ToGetHer Further to connect with women sharing their successes and their setbacks to help women get further together
  https://www.togetherfurther.org
- Attend NOI Club and Blooming Founder events to feel inspired and motivated by other women's accomplishments
  https://www.noiclub.org, https://www.bloomingfounders.org
- Watch Brené Brown's Ted Talk on The Power of

- Vulnerability
  https://www.ted.com/talks/brene_brown_on_vulnerability
- Watch Harriet Minter's Tedx Talk, Proceed Until Apprehended
  https://www.youtube.com/watch?v=gGkdvg76oEg
- Sign up for Harriet Minter's weekly newsletter, Proceed Until Apprehended, for her insightful perspective, inspiration and information about upcoming events relevant to women getting ahead at work *https://tinyletter.com/HarrietMinter/archive*
- Listen to the Badass Women's Hour podcast
  https://itunes.apple.com/gb/podcast/badass-womens-hour/

3 ADDICTED TO INSPIRATION

Attending the Women in Project Management Conference was like a gateway drug – I was immediately hooked and couldn't get enough of that high from being around so many amazing women, hearing such inspiring stories. I signed up for every event I could find – from panel events on 'Breaking the glass ceiling' to full day events run by Marie Claire or Stylist magazine, to motivational speeches on 'Tackling the gender pay gap' – any opportunity for me to potentially meet kindred spirits and find a tribe of likeminded women.

I still hated networking, but at least I now had a purpose – I wanted to connect, to share, to understand, and more importantly, to be understood. I swapped business cards, and added people on LinkedIn. I heard stories of other women's challenges with trying to break into senior management roles, and empathized with the frustration of being mistaken for junior administrative staff, simply due to the misfortune of being a woman in the workplace.

With every event I attended I could feel the benefits of that initial high, but I started to become a more discerning attendee – I would notice and become irked by things like the (male) chair repeatedly interrupting the (female) speakers. Or I would sit patiently in the audience, listening to the interesting speakers and inspired by some of the discussion in the Q&A, but then we would all stand up to leave without getting a chance to speak to the women around us. I found it incredibly frustrating to think of how much wisdom, heartfelt guidance and experience was hidden in the women around me, without an outlet or a safe space for us to truly share and connect on a genuine level. But I shrugged it off at the time, wishing I just had an outlet to share my feedback with the organisers, but they didn't seem to ask the attendees what we thought, if in fact they even wanted to know.

My colleagues continued to be dismissive of these "feminist events" I was attending, but I knew that they were helping to sustain me – I needed that fix in order to keep going. I needed the regular reminder that I wasn't alone, that there were plenty of other women out there struggling just like I was, and that if they had somehow managed to make a success of themselves, then maybe I could do it too.

Lessons I learned from this experience:

- The more events I attended, the more events I learned about - you start with one, and go from there.
- The events I attended didn't all need to be perfect for me to draw inspiration and learning from them - even the most boring or frustrating event could turn out to have a silver lining by connecting with one kindred spirit.
- Draw support from people who understand - my colleagues couldn't see how important these events were to me, so I couldn't draw support from them. Luckily my boyfriend did, and he strongly encouraged me to keep going.

Reflection questions for you:

- What kind of events/gatherings/activities do you find inspiring?
- When did you last attend an event that inspired or motivated you in some way?
- Who would be the best person in your life for you to share your inspiration with?

Useful resources for you:

- Try using Eventbrite (*https://www.eventbrite.co.uk/*) to find events that work for you - start with one and go from there. If you're in London you have a multitude of options, from We Are The City (*https://www.wearethecity.com/*) for more of a corporate focus to the more spiritual outlook of Alternatives events (*https://www.alternatives.org.uk*) to taking a new perspective with Escape the City *(https://www.escapethecity.org/*.

4 FINDING MY VOICE

Long before I reached the end of my 30 day challenge I knew that I wasn't going to be able to let go of that new morning routine. The repetition and structure soothed me – it gave me a sense of certainty and security in a world that otherwise felt completely chaotic. No matter how I slept, and no matter what the weather, I was reassured by the fact that I would wake up every morning to journal, practice yoga and do my Headspace. Then, and only then, would I leave the house to walk my pretty little side-street route to work, accompanied by the inspiring voices from my Ted Talks. I would arrive at work feeling as if I had been in another world – one where inspiring women were in charge, showing me the way to a life of success, and they would stay by my side, silently cheering me on throughout the day.

After a few weeks of my journaling/yoga/Headspace routine I began to notice something strange happening. I would wake up feeling anxious, as usual, and would 'braindump' pages of fear and anxiety in my journal. Then, after practicing my yoga and meditation, I would return to my pages and write again, but this time not only was my handwriting completely different – calmer, neater, more legible – my thoughts were clearer too. Where I was beginning with problems and difficulties, I would return with solutions and options. It was as if I was creating a way to quieten the chaos and listen to myself properly. I began to notice that this quiet little voice was quite wise – whenever I would act on the solutions it proposed, good things would happen. Unexpectedly wonderful things. I didn't know what was happening, but I felt like I'd found something magical within myself.

Looking back now, I know that I had accidentally uncovered my own intuition. My own instincts. My own sense of self. At 32 years of age, I realised I had spent my lifetime struggling with fear and high-functioning anxiety to the extent I had never been able to listen to my own voice. I had been so terrified of being what I thought other people wanted me to be that I hadn't even realised I didn't really know who I was.

It took time for me to gradually learn to fully trust that voice – to know the difference between my Fear and my Intuition. To know how unstable I became when Anxiety was in charge, and to know how to calmly bring myself back into my body before I made any decisions. But this was my awakening.

Lessons I learned from this experience:

- My intuition is my superpower - and I have the ability to harness it.
- I could understand more about what worked for me, or what didn't, and feel empowered to give myself the opportunity to really thrive.
- I could choose to alter my surroundings and my thought processes - by seeking out inspiring female role models I was sending strong messages to myself that I could change my situation for the better.

Reflection questions for you:

- When did you last connect to your intuition? Do you know what helps you to connect with it?
- Do you ever struggle to make decisions? Or look back and regret choices you made, even when you had a feeling it wouldn't work out?
- When did you last make time to sit and listen to what was going on for you?
- When did you last choose to change something about your environment? Whether it's how you get to work, or what your workspace feels like - what one thing could you change today to help you feel more inspired?

Useful resources for you:

- Try making time to switch off from technology in order to reconnect with yourself - ironically there are apps that help you

to do this, like Moment (*https://inthemoment.io/*), which helps you monitor and reduce your screen time. Alternatively you could try turning off your notifications, or go running without music, or try swimming – anything that means you put your phone down temporarily and allow your thoughts to settle.
- Try practising mindfulness in a way that works for you – whether it is by buying yourself a beautiful new journal and pouring out your thoughts, or downloading an app like Happyfeed (*https://www.happyfeed.co/*) to help you practice the art of feeling grateful. Anything that helps you to live in the present moment.
- Try the yogic practice of balanced breathing, explained in the first few minutes of this Yoga With Adriene YouTube video from Day 26 of her True series *(https://www.youtube.com/watch?v=hrVbZIA4hO8&t=320s)*

5 CULTIVATING JOY

One of the benefits of being unhappy in a well-paid job is that you have the means to 'throw money at the problem'. This isn't a sustainable solution, and it doesn't always get you closer to where you want to be, but it does help you to explore your various different curiosities, tapping into parts of yourself that have previously been left dormant or hidden, perhaps for a very long time.

It had been more than 24 years since I had rode a horse, but my fear of their size and strength was completely outweighed by the excitement and gratitude I had for my good fortune in getting to finally have private riding lessons at the age of 32. It seemed like the perfect investment for my generous salary – I'd rather be facing fears and learning new skills than watching my money (quite literally) go down the drain in a pub.

I was blessed with an excellent teacher – Emma was patient but honest and direct, there was no bullshit with her – she spelled out clearly what I needed to learn, for my own sake as well as the horse's, and she gently guided me through the stages of learning to walk, trot and eventually canter competently in the arena. It was the first time in my life that someone had broken steps down so clearly for me, explained why I needed to know what she was telling me, and why it wasn't working for me when I initially tried to implement it. There was nothing personal about the critique, it was matter of fact – this is what the horse can sense, and this is why they are moving in a particular way, or not as the case may be. There was no mocking, shaming or impatience in the way she spoke to me, even though as a complete beginner I'm sure I must have frustrated her at times.

As the weeks passed, I could feel my own progress developing – I didn't need external validation or approval, because the horse's movement beneath me was affirmation enough. My confidence in myself began to grow along with my abilities – it was so refreshing to have this time in the week where I had to completely switch off to the world and be totally focused on the task at hand, feeling the impact of how every little adjustment to my posture and position on the horse had an immediate effect. I would leave each lesson feeling empowered and elated, proud of everything I'd achieved, even if no one else would ever see what I had done.

Contrasting this experience to my working environment, I started to see so clearly why I was frustrated with the existing arrangement – having thrived under Emma's clear instruction, no wonder I was struggling and suffocating under the intense pressure to perform in the office, without any actual guidance as to how to achieve success. It's not that I needed to be micromanaged, more that I needed someone to clearly explain the sequencing of the stages, and my role in successfully achieving them, to give me a safe space to work within.

With the benefit of this awareness, I was then able to cast my mind back to a previous role I'd held, one where I'd not only thrived but succeeded beyond my own expectations – the difference there was the manager I was working with had sat me down at the start of the project, and laid out the stages in a logical order for me, explaining the driving factors for success, and the potential pitfalls to keep an eye out for. They had essentially given me the road map I needed to manage myself and my team.

Looking back now, with the benefit of hindsight, it's always easy to see where things went wrong, or where things could have been done so much better. But learning the ways in which we work well doesn't mean we will always have the good fortune of learning in that way, it just means we'll appreciate it more when we do, and perhaps be a little kinder to ourselves when we don't.

Lessons I learned from this experience:

- There is so much power in understanding how we learn best - by becoming an expert on ourselves we have greater awareness in what will, and won't, work for us.
- We can use hobbies or pastimes to learn more about ourselves, and to help us with understanding how we can work better too.
- The importance of making time to switch off, to connect with our more physical senses, and really trust our instinctual awareness.
- The power of developing and drawing on our own internal affirmation rather than relying on external validation to build up our confidence in ourselves.

Reflection questions for you:

- What hobbies or pastimes do you make time for, and when?
- When did you last allow yourself to simply 'play' or switch off fully?
- Do you know how you learn best? Is it easier for you to read books or see images? Do you prefer to see the process step by step, or be thrown in the deep end?
- When did you last feel so proud of achieving something that you didn't need external validation?

Useful resources for you:

- Try taking some free personality tests to help you explore your strengths and preferred methods of learning -

(*https://www.16personalities.com/free-personality-test*) - they're not to be relied on heavily, but can be helpful in your exploration of your priorities.
- Try creating a document or email folder to capture positive feedback when you receive it, or take screenshots of messages and save them - too often we hold on to criticism but forget to pay attention to praise.
- Read Anne Marie Slaughter's book Unfinished Business about the need for work-life balance, and how it is essential to achieving gender equality.
- Watch Elizabeth Gilbert's Ted Talk on Success, Failure and the Drive to Keep Creating *(https://www.ted.com/talks/elizabeth_gilbert_success_failure_and_the_drive_to_keep_creating)*

Finding My Way: Out of the darkness, into the light

6 CALM BEFORE THE STORM

As the months passed, I was starting to feel more confident in my role – partly thanks to the help of a new mentor I'd sought out within the organization I was working with. I'd always assumed I needed female role models – and I had previously done some great work with a female mentor – but I realised there was also a lot for me to gain from a male perspective. More importantly, there's a lot for me to gain from someone (male or female) who has the right wisdom and experience to support me in my career.

My mentor helped me to map out the project stages, and understand my role, in a way I now know was best for me to learn and implement. But I was beginning to lose sleep again, terrified of taking on the next daunting stage of the project, with the added responsibility and visibility it required.

One challenge that I continue to struggle with is the terror I feel when I'm about to try something for the first time – once I've done it, I'm immediately confident and happy to repeat it, but it's that build up to the very first attempt that paralyses me.

The task mushrooms in my mind, expanding into a very definite public humiliation, with everyone realizing just how little I know, and how badly I've failed. It's cruel, and never true, but I do this to myself every time I'm faced with something brand new.

I've since learned the best way for me to handle this fear is to voice it – particularly to someone who understands what I'm feeling, and won't dismiss it as being irrational.

As I've learned from the work of Brené Brown, empathy is the best antidote to shame. A good mentor, from my experience, understands this, and because they've generally lived through similar experiences to those you're going through, they're able to identify with your challenges in a way that others might struggle with. They're able to empathise and support, rather than sympathise while distance themselves, which our colleagues, and even our friends, may do out of their own discomfort.

I was fortunate enough to have a number of mentors over my time in the corporate world, and they all helped me in different ways. I learned that people are generally very keen to help, and willing to pass on their own experience, if we are only willing to ask.

Lessons I learned from this experience:

- Asking for help was still so difficult, but the more I practiced it, the braver I became.
- There is always an opportunity for me to learn and grow – to let go of perfectionism and fixed mindset thinking.

Reflection questions for you:

- When did you last ask someone to help mentor you?
- When did you last try something new, or allow yourself to fail at something?
- When did you last speak about your fears?

Useful resources for you:

- Read this blog post I wrote about Choosing Your Mentor (*https://togetherfurther.org/2016/03/10/manage-your-mentor/*).
- Find yourself a mentor at Back Yourself Mentoring (*https://www.backyourselfmentoring.com/*), a community of women who are smart and brave while recognising that we are stronger together.
- Watch this short animated video of Brené Brown speaking about empathy (*https://www.youtube.com/watch?v=1Evwgu369Jw*)
- Read Daring Greatly by Brené Brown to help give you the courage to be vulnerable and transform the way you live, love, parent and lead.
- Read Mindset by Carol Dweck to help you to let go of fixed

mindset thinking and embrace a growth mindset to allow you to fail, to learn, and to evolve.

7 CRYING OVER SPILT COFFEE

It had been a manic week but I was holding it all together, and proud of it. Just a few more hours and I would be free to spend the weekend with my sister.

The morning had been unexpectedly stressful – a meeting I had thought was just a simple tick box exercise had almost turned into a boxing match. Being around anger was stressful, and we all felt emotional after the meeting had ended.

I went back to my (male) colleagues to tell them what had happened and I completely misjudged my audience – their loud laughter broke the nervous tension for them, but for me it simply diminished and undermined an already upsetting experience.

I looked around for some emotional support but my female colleagues were busy, so I simply put my head down and got stuck back in, determined to put on a brave face and show how well I could handle a stressful situation.

I held it together for most of the day. Rushing to get everything done so I could allow myself to switch off for the weekend. I was planning to take a half-day on the Monday morning too, to make the most of my sister visiting from Ireland, so it was important I had everything in order.

It was nearly the end of the day – the finishing line was in sight, but my energy levels were waning so I made myself a cup of coffee to keep me going. The last time my sister had visited she had complained that we didn't go out to socialize so I was determined to bring her to a pub that night to meet my friends, rather than go home and crash on the couch, which was what I would much rather have done.

The coffee was in front of me, between me and the keyboard. No idea why I placed it there instead of to my right hand side where it would normally be. But that's where it was – a full mug of coffee gradually cooling as I was suddenly energized by its proximity and was working at a faster pace to get myself out of the office sooner.

I don't know exactly how I did it – I think I bumped against it as I reached for the keyboard, and then worried that I had knocked it I lunged at the mug, sending the entire contents all over my chest, completely staining my light pink shirt! I sat in shock for a few seconds, unsure if I would be able to see the funny side just yet, debating whether to show my colleagues, but there was no hiding it. I turned around from my desk, and stood up to try to get to the bathroom before the tears fell.

On my way there I passed a wonderful female colleague of mine – a truly kind-hearted and supportive friend – I tried to make light of the massive spill spreading across my front, but as I made eye contact with her the tears came. She jumped up and came to the bathroom with me – for the first time that day I didn't feel like I was alone.

I told her about the meeting that morning, how afraid I had been of this man's anger, and how confused I had been as to how it had even come about. And then how I had returned and tried to seek support from my male colleagues but I felt as if they had laughed at me. She was so supportive, so understanding and so empathic that I immediately felt so much better. Just knowing it was ok to feel this way, knowing that it was ok to be scared by anger, that it was understandable that in the midst of all this, and the pressure to leave the office on time so I could meet my sister that I could upturn an entire cup of coffee on myself.

On reflection, I feel like that cup of coffee was a cry for help – that I had tried articulating a need for support to my colleagues but the emotional tension was too much for them. By creating a practical, albeit embarrassing problem, perhaps I was trying to manufacture a situation where people could clearly see I needed help.

I thought that in order to be successful I had to act like nothing bothered me – that resilience was the same as stubborn stoicism. I thought I had to act like the guys if I wanted to get ahead, even if it made me unhappy. I can see now how wrong I was – how I was cutting myself off from so much of my self, trying to fit in rather than allowing myself to take my own place in the world and truly belong.

Lessons I learned from this experience:

- It's so important to be aware of the signs that you might be feeling fragile or needing a little extra support, rather than letting it build up and culminate in an explosion of some kind.
- It's important to know whom to turn to for support, rather than feeling disheartened or frustrated when people are unable to understand or help you with your situation.
- Never underestimate the power of empathy or a kind word. Simply knowing you're not alone in something can make all the difference.
- When you feel like you're rushing to 'power through' something, stop, sit back, and reflect on what's really going on, so you can take better care of yourself.

Reflection questions for you:

- What are the signs that something difficult is bubbling up in you?
- How do you help yourself to check back in or ground yourself in your body?
- Who are your 'go to' people for when you're struggling with something?

Useful resources for you:

- Join a community who will support and understand you, where you know you can reach out and ask for help. I've created my own version of this with ToGetHer Further

(*http://www.togetherfurther.org/*), but you can also find lots of other supportive communities available online or in person, from Driven Woman (*https://drivenwoman.co.uk/*) to Lean In circles (*https://leanin.org/*) and beyond.
- Read Beta: Quiet Girls Can Run The World by Rebecca Holman to help you explore whether 'pushing through' is right for you, and help you define success for yourself on your own terms.
- Read The Heroine's Journey by Maureen Murdock to break down traditional masculine measures of success and embrace more feminine values.

Finding My Way: Out of the darkness, into the light

8 BREAKTHROUGH (OR BREAKDOWN)

I had spent the weekend with my youngest sister, doing my best to entertain her, and generally show her how great it was to live in London, and how well I was doing, or at least, how well I thought I was doing.

We had a whirlwind weekend of drinks with friends, shopping in the City, dinner out in nice restaurants, while still trying to find quality time to catch up. Then all of a sudden it was Monday morning, and I was exhausted.

It was a critical time at work – a key stage in a high value contract about to be let – and I had arranged a half-day on that Monday to spend time with her before she went to the airport.

I spent that morning huddled over my laptop, checking emails and following up on tasks that needed to be completed in order for the project to go ahead as planned that afternoon. I felt powerless and yet guilty for not being in the office – as if my physical presence there would make everyone complete their tasks sooner.

I was supposed to be getting some last few minutes with my sister, and instead I resented her being there, distracting me if only in a small way from something that felt far more important at the time.

Finally it was almost time for her to catch her train, and she assured me she didn't need me to walk her to the station, which gave me at least 30 precious minutes back in my day, easing the painful pressure in a way that almost felt like relief.

And then my sister, my twenty-something but still my baby sister in my eyes, asked me *"Are you ok?"* Before I had the chance to reply, she said, *"Because I'm worried about you, you don't seem happy."*

With that, my emotional floodgates opened, tears streaming down my face, as I tried to comprehend the question, thinking to myself *"Happy? What did happiness have to do with it? Couldn't she see I was successful? And wasn't that good enough? Wasn't that the goal in life?"*

I clearly wasn't happy – far from it – and as I allowed myself to cry openly, and let my not-so-baby sister comfort me, I realised that this was a very odd image of success to be role modelling for her. Surely success meant something more along the lines of doing well at something you care about, not working yourself up into a pent up ball of stress because you're afraid of letting people down?

Those few minutes we spent together were real, and open, and emotional. We connected in a way that made it very hard to say goodbye, but left me determined to make some changes and be a better Big Sister, showing my family, and the world, that I could find a way to be successful that didn't hurt so much.

As I walked to work, trying to refocus on the tasks I needed to face that afternoon, I couldn't help but think of the many amazing women I had met over the years who had struggled in different ways but, like me, had ended up crying on someone's shoulder (often mine) about how frustrating their careers had become, for reasons that felt beyond their control. I felt this rush of anger at the injustice that I had allowed this to happen to myself, and a sudden spark of inspiration that I would somehow find a way to help prevent it happening for other women, and hopefully improve things for myself in the process.

Lessons I learned from this experience:

- How important it is for us to truly define success for ourselves – to take the time to reflect and understand what exactly it is we want from life, rather than going along with what we think we're supposed to want.
- The power of being truly real, open and vulnerable, allowing others to support you, and enabling you to connect on a deeper and more meaningful level.
- That even the most negative, upsetting, heart-breaking experience has the potential to be turned into a positive opportunity to benefit ourselves and others.

Reflection questions for you:

- What does success really look like for you? Allow yourself to take some time to think about what is genuinely important to you. What brings you alive? What are the things you must do or achieve before you die?
- When did you last let yourself be truly open and vulnerable with someone you can trust?
- Is there anything you're struggling with at the moment that you might be able to channel into a solution to benefit yourself and others who may be suffering?

Useful resources for you:

- Watch Emilie Wapnick's Ted Talk on Why Some of Us Don't Have One True Calling

(*https://www.ted.com/talks/emilie_wapnick_why_some_of_us_don_t_have_one_true_calling*)
- Try creating a Vision Board for yourself – either by physically using a notice board or starting with a Pinterest version (*http://www.pinterest.co.uk/*) – this will help you to connect with how you want to feel and define a life you truly love.
- Try using this Big Vision Guided Visualisation Script (*http://www.creativity-portal.com/articles/jennifer-lee/big-vision-visualization-script.html#.WoGLbZOFjeQ*) – for you to record in your own voice. You can do this using the Voice Memo recording app on your phone. It will help you to let go of reality as it currently is, and allow you to dream bigger, defining success for yourself.
- Watch Amy Purdy's Ted Talk on Living Beyond Limits to draw inspiration from life's obstacles (*https://www.ted.com/talks/amy_purdy_living_beyond_limits*).
- Read Big Magic by Elizabeth Gilbert to embrace creative living beyond fear.
- Listen to the Magic Lessons podcast by Elizabeth Gilbert exploring creative living with special guests, including Brené Brown and Amy Purdy (*https://www.elizabethgilbert.com/magic-lessons/*)

Finding My Way: Out of the darkness, into the light

9 MAGICAL MOMENT

It had been a few weeks since my emotional breakthrough, and I knew I wanted to do something to help women at work, but still had no idea what I would do, or what it would even look like, until one Friday afternoon I saw something that made inspiration burst out of me before I'd even realised what was happening.

I had been working on the project for less than a year, and it was an intense environment for everyone concerned. The client organization appeared to be run in a strict hierarchy, and seemed to rely heavily on blame culture to keep everyone in line. I found the macho attitude overwhelming, and was frustrated by the repressed silence throughout the office. At times the air would feel stiff and heavy with tension.

To help with the anxiety I had been experiencing at work, I had been busily seeking out female allies throughout the office – in various roles and functions, and from different organisations – I wanted to find women who felt as frustrated as I did, but determined to do something to make a difference.

One of my close friends had been struggling for quite some time – an extremely intelligent, highly qualified young woman – she had been wasting away in a junior administrative role waiting for the opportunities for development that had apparently been promised to her at interview stage. A recent attempt to apply for a role in another department had been blocked by her current manager – he seemed to be taking offence by the fact that she wanted to change teams. (It may or may not be relevant that my friend was an extremely attractive, friendly young woman.) The situation quickly escalated and my friend went from wasting away in an under-utilised role to what looked like being punished for wanting to progress.

It hurt me to see her like this, and I was doing everything I could to help from an external perspective – whether it was being a shoulder to cry on, or proof-reading her (extremely impressive) CV, or sending her new job opportunities for her to apply to and move on from this unhappy situation. I also spoke to a few senior women I knew across various organisations to gain their insight and see if they could help in some way, and they offered various forms of advice and assistance in return.

For a while it seemed to be getting even worse – the Human Resources team didn't seem to be helping her at all, and if anything seemed to be implying that she was the one causing the trouble in the first instance, which seriously pushed my buttons. It was looking like they were going to find a way to let her go, which would at least have been a way out for her but felt like an unfair ending to a very unhappy situation, particularly given the way her reputation was being left in tatters.

And then, just when it seemed like all hope was lost, one of the senior females in the organization offered to take her under their wing – for her to interview for a junior role under them, but a role with far more progression and learning opportunities than she was currently receiving. She was also offering to mentor her, to help build up her confidence again, and to restore her faith in the organization, as well as their faith in her in return. It was magical. Not just for them, but for the message it sent to the whole office. That this senior manager was willing to put her head above the parapet, to reject the negative opinions that seemed to have been maliciously spread about this young woman with so much potential, and to offer her a lifeline in a time of crisis, regardless of how this may affect her own standing in the organization. Wow. Just wow. It looked like such a selfless, inspiring, magical act of kindness. She didn't have to do that. She could have just kept her head down and ignored the whole thing. She didn't need to get involved. But she did.

And she sent a ripple. A magical ripple that I felt so powerfully that I jumped up from my desk and went to speak to both of them individually, delighted and relieved that some good had come from all of this mess. Happy to have had any part in bringing them together, and so inspired to see women helping each other to get ahead at work. And with that, a spark of inspiration appeared inside me and grew until the energy was rushing through my body.

I sat back down at my desk determined to write something to capture this moment for posterity. Something to share what I had felt to let more women know about this feeling in the hopes they would experience it too.

I needed an outlet – a website, something like a free blog would do for now – I just needed a name. I kept thinking about how amazing it was when women helped each other like that, and how if only we all worked together then think of how much easier life would be, and how much further we would get as well. The words 'further' and 'together' jumped out at me because they both contained the word 'her', and I wondered if I could overlay them somehow in a way that made sense....

And so, on the 26th February 2016, ToGetHer Further was born.

This is what poured out of me that afternoon in the very first blog post:

"According to former U.S. Secretary of State, Madeline Albright, "there is a special place in hell for women who don't help other women". Conversely, I believe there should be a special place in heaven for those who do. And I want to earn my place in that illustrious group of awesome women. Hence this blog. I want to create a support network to provide useful, relevant information to women who want to further their careers. Whether you're a student or a new graduate about to enter the workforce, or you're an experienced professional who wants to learn how to negotiate your salary, or you want to re-train entirely, or you want to set up your own business – I want to help point you in the right direction. Let's work together to get each other that little bit further."

Lessons I learned from this experience:

- The importance of surrounding yourself with allies who support you at work.
- The powerful magic that happens when women help other women.
- Done is better than perfect – just start creating and see what happens.

Reflection questions for you:

- When did you last find someone at work you could rely on?
- When did you last see a woman help another woman out at work?
- When was the last time you did something to help a woman at work?
- When did you last share an inspiring story about women helping women?

Useful resources for you:

- Join a community of women and embrace the support of your sisterhood: ToGetHer Further (*http://www.togetherfurther.org/*), NOI Club (*http://www.noiclub.org/*), Blooming Founders (*http://www.bloomingfounders.org/*), Lean In (*http://www.leanin.org/*), Driven Woman (*http://www.drivenwoman.co.uk/*) and beyond.
- Listen to the Badass Women's Hour podcast with Harriet

Minter, Emma Sexton and Natalie Campbell (*https://itunes.apple.com/gb/podcast/badass-womens-hour/*)
- Listen to the Guilty Feminist podcast with Deborah Frances-White & guests to hear discussions on the big topics all 21st century feminists agree on, whilst confessing our "buts" – the insecurities, hypocrisies and fears that undermine our lofty principles (*http://guiltyfeminist.com/*)
- Read How to be a Woman by Caitlin Moran, for a feminist awakening.
- Read Everywoman by Jess Phillips to hear one woman's truth about speaking the truth, including a touching tribute to the many women who have supported her along the way.
- Read Nasty Women – a collection of essays and accounts on what it is to be a woman in the 21st Century.
- Read Lean In by Sheryl Sandberg, if you haven't already, and for balance, read Lean Out by Dawn Foster.
- Watch these amazing Ted Talks from Sheryl Sandberg, Susan Cain, Verna Myers, Susan Colantuono and Anne-Marie Slaughter (*https://www.theguardian.com/women-in-leadership/2015/may/27/five-ted-talks-that-will-change-the-way-you-work*).

10 FINDING MY TRIBE

Sharing that first blog post on my personal Facebook page was nerve-wracking yet exciting – I was terrified of putting myself out there to potentially be judged or ridiculed, but I took that first leap of faith, somehow knowing that I would reach women who would catch me, and one by one, they appeared.

We spend so much of our lives trying to fit in, to be like everyone else, afraid of looking different or standing out in case it opens us up to judgement or embarrassment, but by doing that we're hiding our true selves from sight, not letting anyone ever know who we really are.

Posting that first blog was my statement to the world that I was interested in helping women to help other women, and that I cared about it so much that I was willing to be vulnerable and take the risks that went with putting myself out there so openly.

By being brave, and putting myself out there, my friend Jane saw exactly what I was trying to do, and immediately put me in touch with her friend Paola Garbini, founder of NOI

Club – a community of female achievers, supporting each other turn their passions into successes.

I was inspired by what Paola was doing already, but also nervous that maybe the world already had enough women's groups, so maybe there wouldn't be room for ToGetHer Further after all. But Paola put all those fears to rest and she championed me and my little blog – encouraging me to keep learning, and growing and believing in myself, reassuring me that there was room for everyone, and the more communities that existed to support women, the better. She believed in me and my abilities more than I did myself.

The first NOI Club event I ever attended was a full day retreat at the Good Enough Club in London – this felt so aptly named and timed because I had only recently stumbled upon the works of Brené Brown, through one of my many morning Ted Talks, and had recently begun reading her book, The Gifts of Imperfection, which discusses the concept of being 'good enough' at length.

The event itself was wonderful, magical even, and I did my best to capture this in the blog post I wrote afterwards (*https://togetherfurther.org/2016/06/20/event-noi-club-retreat/*). I took so many lessons away, and made so many new connections, but again, the biggest gift Paola gave me was the reassurance that it doesn't matter if something has already been done, or written, or created, that there is space for us all to invent and reinvent ourselves and our purpose, but we must then be brave and share it with the world, for us all to benefit.

I left that NOI event a true champion of the club, and of everything Paola was doing for women – I had already been encouraging friends to join her Facebook group, but now I was attending every event I possibly could. The NOI events were different to those I'd attended across London before – I didn't have to network, I could be myself. I wasn't just making contacts, I was making heartfelt connections, and even friendships.

It was that first NOI event where I met Vix Anderton, founder of The Practical Balance
(*https://www.thepracticalbalance.com/*), who continues to impress, inspire and support me to this day.

It was at the NOI Mirror event later that year that I met Esther Zimmer (*http://estherzimmer.com/*) and Hannah Smith (*https://tinyletter.com/ConversationsWithVanGogh/archive*) – two women who bravely bare their beautiful souls in their writing, and inspire me to be more honest in how I live my life.

It was at the NOI Christmas party that I met Priya Dabasia and Jenny Corrie of Being ManKind
(*http://www.beingmankind.org/*) an amazing initiative aimed at highlighting more authentic role models for modern young men, breaking down stereotypes to facilitate gender equality. I was very aware that my passion was for helping women, so it inspired me to meet people who were passionate about helping men, keen for us to support each other, and maybe find a way to work together someday.

The list could go on indefinitely – there are so many women I have met online and in person through NOI Club and their events – women who have helped me on a practical level to get my finances in order or successfully apply for a trademark for ToGetHer Further or have connected with me on a personal level through our journeys to full mental health following painful childhood experiences.

I didn't know then exactly what I was going to do with ToGetHer Further, but being in NOI Club showed me that anything was possible, and having Paola's support gave me hope that someday it would all become clear, that all the pieces would finally fall into place. Regardless of where I was going, I knew the journey would be easier with so many amazing women by my side.

Lessons I learned from this experience:

- The power of female collaboration and community when you're in a safe, non-judgemental, non-competitive space.
- That there's room for us all to bring our ideas to the table – even if we're afraid it's already been done, we can bring our own unique perspective to the world.
- The amazing benefit of having people believe in you, support you and encourage you to keep going.

Reflection questions for you:

- When did you last publicly speak about something you're interested in? Or share a reference to it on social media?
- Have you ever had ideas for businesses/goods/services that you dismissed because you thought they'd already been done?
- What do you think the world needs more of, even if it does exist already? What would you do differently to make it better?

Useful resources for you:

- Join a community of women from ToGetHer Further, to NOI Club, or Blooming Founders, to Lean In, or Driven Woman.
- Attend a NOI Club event to connect with other women and become inspired.
- Attend an Escape the City event to allow yourself to see the world from a fresh perspective (*https:/www.escapethecity.org*).
- Watch Elizabeth Gilbert's Ted Talk on Your Elusive Creative Genius (*https://www.ted.com/talks/elizabeth_gilbert_on_genius*)

- Watch Simon Sinek's Ted Talk on How Great Leaders Inspire Action
  (*https://www.ted.com/talks/simon_sinek_how_great_leaders_inspire_action*)
- Watch Adam Grant's Ted Talk on The Surprising Habits of Original Thinkers
  (*https://www.ted.com/talks/adam_grant_the_surprising_habits_of_original_thinkers*)

11 (RELUCTANTLY) EMBRACING CREATIVITY

My least favourite session of the NOI retreat had been the one on Creativity – even the idea of it made me uncomfortable, but I went along with Rachel's guidance as our facilitator to see what I would learn from the experience. The biggest learning outcome I took from the session, and quickly, was just how strong my resistance was to anything creative. It didn't matter that I had been blogging for months, or that I enjoyed baking or knitting or gardening, I was reluctant to take on a label of being creative in any way.

When Rachel asked us to line ourselves up in order of how creative we thought we were, from 1 – 10, I immediately went to stand where I thought 0 would be. I was proudly defiant, arrogantly telling the room of amazing women: "I'm not creative, I'm a project manager, I get sh*t done!" Oh it pains me to remember how ignorant I was back then – I thought I could hide behind a shield of productivity, that no one could make me feel vulnerable or open to judgement if I was simply efficient and didn't take the risk of daring to be creative.

To her immense credit, Rachel simply smiled knowingly at those of us who rejected our creative side, and encouraged us to make the time to read Big Magic, by Elizabeth Gilbert, who I knew of from her Eat Pray Love fame. But I was in the middle of my Brené Brown awakening, devouring The Gifts of Imperfection, so it took a few months before I followed Rachel's advice, and began the process of truly embracing my creative side. In fact, it was only thanks to my interest in Brené that I found my way back to Elizabeth Gilber and her Magic Lessons on creativity.

I'd stumbled upon Brené Brown on one of my walks to work and immediately became a huge fan – I was kicking myself when I realised my Mum had given me a copy of her book over three years earlier, but I'd left it languishing on my shelf, gathering dust all this time. I'd like to think we read things when we're ready for them, and I was so ready for Brené's work when I finally took the plunge. Even the opening paragraph of the introductory chapter had me in tears:

"Wholehearted living...means cultivating the courage, compassion, and connection to wake up in the morning and think, No matter what gets done and how much is left undone, I am enough. It's going to bed at night thinking, Yes, I am imperfect and vulnerable and sometimes afraid, but that doesn't change the truth that I am also brave and worthy of love and belonging."

To say this piece blew my mind would be an understatement – it was if she had reached into the depths of my soul and dragged me kicking and screaming into the light. I shed so many tears as I read and re-read her words, feeling layers of judgements and fears peel away with every passing page. It was as if someone had given me permission to let go, to sit down, to rest a while. To stop forcing myself to forge on and push through the pain, but to simply sit, listen and let myself be. Just as I am. Even now as I remember how awestruck I was by her work – how clearly she painted this picture of all the ways I'd erroneously previously defined success, and how ignorant I'd been of the many ways we humans need to allow ourselves to revive and thrive in the world – my heart aches for how lost I had been up until this point. For how much of a journey I would find myself taking.

I became obsessed with all of Brené's work – soaking up every drop I could find, from books to podcasts – which is how I found her Magic Lesson with Elizabeth Gilbert, continuing her work from her book Big Magic through a series of interviews. During the podcast, Brené mocked herself for her past ignorance and arrogance in denying her creativity, saying playfully "I don't have time for A-R-T, I've got a J-O-B!" Hearing her describe her challenges with creativity in such a similar way to how I'd done at the NOI event was earth shattering. I physically felt the impact. As if someone had smashed the illusion I'd held dear that by holding onto my productivity I could avoid potential pain in owning my creativity. Oh wow!

She went on to say that people who struggled to own their creativity generally had some sort of shameful incident in their distant past where they had allowed themselves to be vulnerable and been knocked back for their efforts. I tried to shake this off, to dismiss it as something that wasn't relevant to me, when suddenly a memory came flooding back to me painfully clearly – me, as a teenager, writing an overly-enthusiastic essay about how I wanted to be a writer when I grew up, only to receive a low mark and an implied message to give up while I still could. Remembering that experience still stung, almost 20 years later.

Suddenly all these visions came to me, of how I used to write poems and create little books of stories when I was a child, and how I would write creative little works of fiction in my early adolescence – submitting them to a supportive teacher who would indulge me in reading my extra work, encouraging me to continue on my creative path. But that poor mark, accompanied by unsupportive feedback calling me out on my amateurish skills hurt so much that it stopped me in my tracks. I wracked my brain trying to remember if I'd even attempted a piece of creative writing since that day, and I couldn't think of a single time.

I'd created my blog as an outlet for my passion to help women – not as a method of exploring a long-lost love of writing – but I inadvertently opened up a reserve of creativity that I'd been denying myself for decades. Now my obstinacy made sense – my refusal to own and identify with this side of myself, afraid of opening myself to further critique, shame or disappointment. Safer to avoid it altogether; to pretend I never wanted it in the first place. Less of chance of failure that way. Even if I was sacrificing my happiness and my true sense of self in return.

Well, not any more.

Finally, I was ready to read Big Magic and embark on my journey towards owning my creativity, and embracing my love of writing, at long last.

Lessons I learned from this experience:

- How cut off I had been from my own sense of creativity.
- How much joy and beauty there is in allowing myself the freedom to explore my creative side.
- How much fear comes up in me – in us all –when we are in danger of feeling vulnerable to criticism or judgement.
- How we always have a choice to learn, grow, and change our paths, no matter how long we've been lost.

Reflection questions for you:

- What does the word 'creativity' mean to you? Is it something you embrace or something you resist strongly like I did?
- When was the last time you did something creative? (Include anything where you made something that didn't exist, from baking to music to art to writing to knitting to gardening to dance and beyond. Anything that you did for the joy or beauty of it rather than the sense of productivity.)
- How do you feel when you allow yourself time to be creative in some way?

Useful resources for you:

- Read the blog post I wrote about Playing with Creativity (*https://togetherfurther.org/2017/02/27/escape-playing-with-creativity/*).
- Read Big Magic and listen to the Magic Lessons podcast by Elizabeth Gilbert – particularly Episode 12 with Brené Brown

(*https://www.elizabethgilbert.com/magic-lessons/*,
https://soundcloud.com/riverheadbooks/ep-12-big-strong-magic)
- Watch Elizabeth Gilbert's Ted Talks on Creativity, if you haven't already
(*https://www.ted.com/speakers/elizabeth_gilbert*)
- If you have any interest in writing, listen to the Beautiful Writer's Podcast by Linda Sivertsen in conversation with published authors (*http://www.beautifulwriterspodcast.com/*)
- Watch Marie Forleo with Cheryl Strayed on How To Become a Writer (*https://www.youtube.com/watch?v=oINfXbPsVqM*).
- Explore options for taking small steps like trying adult colouring books to help you to connect to your creative side, then perhaps work up to something bigger.

12 ABSOLUTE CLARITY

After many months of gradually dissipating fear, I finally reached a pivotal moment in my career – I had achieved the milestone I had been most terrified of facing in the project, and successfully managed the procurement process for a multi-million pound contract. It was as if I'd reached the summit of a torturous mountain, and I was oh so ready for my reward. The accolades poured in from clients and colleagues alike – it was wonderful to finally get the acknowledgement I felt I deserved. And yet, something didn't feel right. The experience felt hollow. I had been afraid for so long, terrified that I would mess this up, and yet now that I was here, having successfully delivered what I'd been tasked to do, I just felt empty. Was this it? Was this what I had been so afraid of? Was this what success felt like? Is this as good as it gets?

I felt so frustrated that I had allowed something to intimidate me for so long only to realise it was simply another stage in learning, and nothing to really get so worked up about. I felt disappointed that achieving what should have felt like a momentous milestone simply felt disheartening. It wasn't enough. I wanted more than this. Especially now that I knew how passionate I was about ToGetHer Further – I felt far more excited at the prospect of turning that into a full time business than I had ever felt about my corporate career. I had no idea how I would do it, but somehow I knew it would all become clear when I was ready.

Just a few short months later, after allowing myself to dive in and explore my creative side, I found myself suddenly experiencing a burst of pure clarity:

"I know what I need to do! I know I need to quit my job — I can't get my head around everything I want to achieve with ToGetHer Further while I'm still working in the corporate world! I need to break free!"

The words came pouring out of me all in a rush but they felt like the truest words I'd ever spoken. They were coming from somewhere deep inside me, somewhere real, and primal, beyond clear consciousness. Somehow I just knew that being in the office every day was stifling my creativity, that I didn't know where my journey was taking me but I did know, with absolute certainty, that I wasn't going to find it staying where I was.

My words excited me — I felt alive with the prospect of so much potential. So much freedom! But I can imagine they terrified my boyfriend. We had just bought a house and tied ourselves into 25 years of mortgage repayments — now was not the time to quit my job and throw caution to the wind — we had strict financial commitments to uphold. I tried to reassure him, to placate him, that I wasn't about to do anything foolish, that of course I would think all of this through and I wouldn't do anything rash. But my words were true. I knew they were. I knew this was going to be my reality, that someday very soon I was going to walk out of work, never to return.

I tried to reassure myself as well — that this wouldn't take too long, that I could figure out how to take steps towards this amazing new life. I gave myself permission to design exactly how I wanted my life to be right now – I couldn't just quit the next day, I needed savings to make sure that the mortgage would be paid. I decided I would like to work part-time for a while, that this would give me time to explore my more creative side, but still with the routine and financial security of consistent income. I didn't think my boss would ever go for this but I didn't let it deter my fantasising. I mapped out a little dream world – one where I handed over some of my projects, then worked part time for a few months, built up some savings, and finished off my role in time to launch my new business, whatever that looked like. It made me feel better even to just imagine this possibility, regardless of how remote the reality may have been.

> **Lessons I learned from this experience:**
>
> - The importance of understanding your priorities, your motivations, and how you truly define success, because if you let others define it for you, you'll end up disappointed.
> - The value in allowing yourself to dream – to explore what you might want from life, giving yourself the freedom to dream big and create infinite opportunities.
> - The importance of trusting and listening to your intuition, and then taking the practical steps to create a reality around your vision.

> **Reflection questions for you:**
>
> - When did you last feel truly motivated and inspired in your work?
> - When did you last feel as if you had a meaningful purpose to your work?
> - Have you ever felt that rush of inspiration and excitement, only to dismiss it as a fantasy? What if you were to allow yourself to tap back into that vision now? What would it look like?

> **Useful resources for you:**
>
> - Read this blog post and exercise from Denise Duffield-Thomas to help you to visualise your Dream Day (*https://luckybitch.com/describe-your-ideal-day-this-will-change-your-life/*).
> - Try creating a Vision Board for yourself

(*https://www.huffingtonpost.com/elizabeth-rider/the-scientific-reason-why_b_6392274.html*) - either by physically using a notice board or starting with a Pinterest (*http://www.pinterest.co.uk/*) version - if you haven't already.
- Try recording your own version of this Big Vision Guided Visualisation Script (*http://www.creativity-portal.com/articles/jennifer-lee/big-vision-visualization-script.html#.WoGLbZOFjeQ*) - to help you visualise where you want your life to take you.
- Watch this Ted Talk by Cleo Wade on How to Change the World by first being brave enough to care (*https://www.ted.com/talks/cleo_wade_want_to_change_the_world_start_by_being_brave_enough_to_care*).

Finding My Way: Out of the darkness, into the light

13 ENOUGH IS ENOUGH IS ENOUGH

While all this inspiring, earth-changing activity had been happening for me, I'd continued to muddle my way through the various challenges I faced in the office. Little by little the fear had dissipated and my confidence and belief in myself was increasing. But I was starting to feel overwhelmed with my workload, and I didn't know how to ask for help. My natural instinct was to lay it all out, to say how overstretched and under-supported I felt, to ask for my load to be lightened, in the hopes that someone would make my job easier for me. Thankfully I met someone who showed me a different, and more effective way.

I met Roxanne through inauspicious circumstances – a member of her team had come to work for me temporarily and we had clashed horribly, I won't get into the details here but you can read about it in a blog post I shared afterwards (https://togetherfurther.org/2016/06/08/feeling-like-a-fraud/). Despite the controversy and conflict, I had been impressed by Roxanne's awareness, maturity and professionalism throughout – especially when she offered her services to me as a mentor, after everything we'd just gone through. It is a true sign of integrity and capability when someone can see you at your worst and still have faith in your ability to learn, grow and succeed from a difficult situation.

Feeling frustrated and lost I went to Roxanne for guidance, hoping she would reassure me that I was handling things the best way possible. Firmly, but kindly, she set me straight. I'd been treating the problem on an emotional level, and that simply wasn't going to be effective in changing my situation. She very quickly explained to me that no matter how nice my boss is, he's not going to want me to bring him problems he's unable to solve, nor is he likely to feel comfortable in the face of intense (female) emotions. It's also highly likely he would interpret the word 'overwhelm' as a statement of my incompetence or lack of ability to cope. She encouraged me to step back from my situation and reframe it in a less personal way – to look at it logically and rationally rather than letting my emotions take over completely – essentially, to try reposition my 'overwhelming problem' as more of a 'financial opportunity'. This was so far from my realm of understanding that it almost felt inauthentic for me to communicate in this way, but I could quickly see how taking this approach could be far more effective than any of my previous honest but emotional attempts had been.

I felt nervous sending the email to my boss, but I also felt much clearer in what I was trying to achieve – it wasn't that I was incompetent, or lazy, or not up to a challenge, I was simply one woman, and I had taken on too much. But rather than pleading for help, I was simply stating in a factual way that I was going to refocus my efforts on what I knew was within my scope of works, while highlighting all of this additional work I'd been worrying about and struggling to do (without reward), as an opportunity for my organisation to add resource and secure additional fees from our client. It wasn't my problem to fix everything, and it wasn't on me to make sure everything got done, all I could do was identify my role, and my capacity, and then make it clear I wasn't going to prioritise or take on anything outside of those clear boundaries.

That said, it's easier to type that in an email than it is to back it up in person. But at least my boss knew the tide was turning – he could see my back was up and I wasn't going to take on any more work for free, not without a fight.

Finally, I reached complete breaking point – enough was enough was enough. I had been through so much on this project, and given so much of my energy and sanity to trying to do a good job, and make so many people happy, but I had finally reached my limit. Having made it clear what I knew was and wasn't my responsibility, I was stubbornly resistant to taking anything else on, regardless of what anyone thought of me at this stage.

I was sitting in a meeting room, listening to the client team casually tell me about an additional package of work I would be managing, while my temperature began to rise sharply, and my hands began to grip the table firmly. I tried to remain as polite as possible, gently interrupting to inquire whether this decision had been agreed formally, looking to my boss for reassurance that he was going to explain things to our client in a way they understood, but I was merely placated, and brushed off with platitudes. I somehow managed to stay in the room until the end of the meeting but I was absolutely seething. I had to get up and walk out of the office afterwards in an attempt to calm myself down. I felt so underappreciated, and undervalued, and simply not understood. It was all I could do to stop myself from quitting right there and then – the only thing that held me back was the knowledge that my savings had recently been obliterated by our new mortgage, so I was going to need some time to build up a buffer before I could walk out the door.

I hated feeling trapped – as if the only reason I was there was to earn money, that's never been a good motivator for me.

I want to work hard and do a good job, but I felt so resentful of being taken for granted – I didn't want to have to say no, or put such firm boundaries in place, and I resented anyone forcing me to do this. I wanted them to read my mind and know what I wanted, so I would never have to be vulnerable by putting myself out there and asking for my needs to be met.

I tried to calm myself down over the next couple of days, reassuring myself that with Roxanne's help I would find a way to make it clear to my boss I would not be taking on additional work, and in the interim I could appease myself by buying nice things with the salary I was earning given I was still gainfully employed.

I was on my way to meet my boyfriend for dinner one Friday night, scrolling mindlessly through Facebook, when out jumped a post from Elizabeth Gilbert on her public writer's page – she was going to be running a Creativity Workshop in Brooklyn, in just over a month's time. I felt this rush of energy flow through me and I clicked on the link to find out more, excited about the prospect of spending a day with a woman who had so recently unleashed an avalanche of creativity within me. But as I looked through the details, I found myself thinking "If only I could go to something like this…" To which I responded immediately with "Why not me?! Why can't I go to something like this?!"

In fact, this felt like the perfect opportunity to do something nice for myself as a reward for staying in a job I wasn't happy in – a worthwhile investment in a happier future. It also worked out well that I had a friend living in Manhattan who had recently invited me to visit, so all of this felt like a clear sign that it was exactly the right thing for me to do. By the time I sat down in the restaurant opposite my boyfriend, I'd already bought my ticket to the workshop and was in the process of researching flights to New York. Oh, and the next day, my friend replied to my news saying she was delighted I was coming to visit, particularly as she had already signed up for the same workshop too, before I'd even mentioned it. Another sign that reassured me I was doing the right thing.

I went back into work that Monday feeling lighter and more excited about my prospects – I had this amazing new adventure on the horizon, and pieces of my puzzle were finally falling into place, even if I had no idea where all of this was leading me. I knew that my current situation was temporary, and that one day in the near future I would finally be doing my own thing, if I could just be patient and hold on a little longer. So it was to my immense frustration that I faced a boss that morning who seemed to be delighting in telling me about the additional work he wanted to add to my load. I went on a lunch break with my good friend Nadia, unburdening myself of my woes, complaining that he didn't understand me at all, that he had no idea that I didn't want more work, if anything I wanted less. Suddenly, the penny dropped – I realised I had been waiting for him to read my mind, I'd never explained to him that I had interests outside of work, and that I had recently come to the clear conclusion that I wanted to leave the corporate world and become my own boss – why on earth would he know that? If anything, he probably did think he was doing me a favour by securing more work for me – usually people enjoy the prospect of longer-term employment.

I walked back into the office terrified but determined to be honest with my boss about what my intentions were around work. I even sat down and wrote out what I was planning to say to help me to get my thoughts clear. My voice shook at first, and my insides were cramping, but somehow I managed to thank him for everything he was doing to try to give me extra work, but to clarify that actually, I didn't want to be on the project long-term, that I'd discovered interests outside of work that I was really passionate about and wanted to explore further, like my writing. I then found myself saying that I'd thought about the three projects I was currently managing, and

I knew that one was coming to a natural conclusion soon, but that another would make more sense if it was reassigned to my colleague who was more strategically aligned and better positioned to manage it, which would leave me with just one project, that I knew I could manage part-time, if they'd allow me to. I proposed working four days a week in the New Year, transitioning to three days a week once the situation had stabilised, which would allow me to explore my outside interest but still build up a financial buffer for when my project eventually ended.

To my complete relief and delight, he didn't immediately say no. He was slightly shocked, but more bemused – I had clearly taken him by surprise. He appreciated my honesty, and was intrigued by my desire to do something so different, but he couldn't agree instantly – he'd have to think it over, which was completely fair and reasonable. I can't remember much after that, I was just shocked and elated that I had managed to be brave enough to say so much – in fact, at one point I had even said the words "I want to be a writer!" Madness. But it hadn't ended badly, if anything it had gone better than I could ever have imagined. I felt this huge weight lift off my shoulders, as if I could stop pretending at last – I could finally own the fact that I no longer felt like I fit in in the corporate world, and maybe now I could fully open myself up to what other possibilities lay waiting for me out there.

> **Lessons I learned from this experience:**
>
> - People genuinely cannot read your mind. If you want them to know something, you need to take the time to think about it, be clear on it, then find the right opportunity to discuss it with them.
> - It's important to be clear about what you want so you can work your way towards being brave enough to ask for it. But if you don't know what that is, then how can you ever get what you want?
> - When I feel resentment and bitterness rising up in me, it's because I feel like I'm not protecting my boundaries well, and I'm doing more than I'm willing or able to do. Rather than taking that out on other people, I now recognise this as a sign that I need to step back and reflect on what feels right for me.
> - My way of communicating is not necessarily the most effective way of being heard or understood. If I'm hesitating over saying something then I need to listen to that hesitation and seek alternative perspectives from someone who might be able to help me to reframe the situation.

> **Reflection questions for you:**
>
> - Do you ever feel annoyed with other people for 'making' you do something? Have you ever tried politely declining, or finding a way to explain why it doesn't feel right for you do something?
> - How do your 'buttons' get pressed? What do you know annoys you quickly and is sure to get a negative reaction from you? What can you do to diffuse that situation before it escalates?
> - When did you last take the time to think about a challenging situation and plan out an alternative reality?
> - When was the last time you tried reframing a challenging

situation from another person's perspective? How would it feel to try that now?

Useful resources for you:

- Watch Adam Grant's Ted Talk on Givers and Takers in the workplace (*https://www.ted.com/talks/adam_grant_are_you_a_giver_or_a_taker/*).
- Watch Scott Dinsmore's Ted Talk How to Find Work You Love (*https://www.ted.com/talks/scott_dinsmore_how_to_find_work_you_love*).
- Watch Harriet Lerner's Ted Talk on Why Won't He Apologize to help gain new perspective in reframing situations of disagreement or conflict (*https://www.youtube.com/watch?v=5r6Y9uhmL6Y*).
- Read The Dance of Anger and The Dance of Connection by Harriet Lerner to help you get fresh perspective on frustrating situations or relationships that are really pushing your buttons.
- Read The Gifts of Imperfection by Brené Brown.

14 ESCAPING THE CITY

I'd heard a lot about Escape the City over the previous year – my friend Jane had met Paola when they were both on the Start Up Tribe in 2015, and lots of the women in NOI Club were graduates of the various schemes available through Escape. I'd been arrogantly dismissive when I first heard about their services – cockily believing I already knew what kind of business I wanted to create, and I didn't need to pay someone lots of money to teach me that over the course of three months... But if I'd learned anything from all the Ted Talks, books, and inspiring speakers I'd come across over the previous year, it was that you were never really finished learning.

As soon as my boss officially approved my plan to go part-time, it all started to feel very real, and very scary. I began to worry about how I would manage to be productive in building ToGetHer Further into a business if I was at home, all by myself. I had painful memories of studying alone at home while at University, and was afraid that 'the darkness' might descend if I was left alone for long periods of time. And so, I entertained the notion of participating in one of the Escape Tribes, not necessarily for the education, but more for the support of a likeminded community. I thought it would be helpful to be surrounded by other people going through the same process as I was, rather than the dubious looks on my colleagues' faces when I told them I was essentially quitting my job (eventually) without another job to go to.

There were two Tribe options available – one to help you build a business, the other to help you learn more about yourself, to align your strengths and values to live a more authentic life. Although I "knew" I wanted to build ToGetHer Further into a business, I was also very much aware that I had only recently realised how much I loved writing, so I was intrigued to discover what else I might learn about myself, given the opportunity. I'd also recently realised that the work I wanted to do to help women was not too dissimilar to coaching services, so I was curious to explore whether that might be an avenue for me to explore further as well. I spoke to friends of mine who had undertaken either of the Tribe schemes, to gauge my own sense of intuition, and eventually went with the more introspective 'Get Unstuck' option, which they've since reformulated and renamed the Career Change Accelerator.

It was a 12-week course when I embarked on my Escape journey, and it turned out to be one of the most intense, educational, frustrating yet enlightening periods of my life. So much came up in me unexpectedly, from revelations about who I am, and how I see myself, to challenges with relationships and friendships – new and old – to facing fears and expanding my comfort zone. It was as if we were breaking ourselves down in order to build ourselves anew.

In the first week of the Tribe, we were invited to begin the process of volunteering for a five minute Open Mic slot that would be held at the end of every evening we met. The thought of impending dread weighing over me every week for the 12-week programme terrified me so much that I volunteered immediately for the very first slot – better to rip the plaster off and be done with it.

Anxious about wanting to say 'the right thing', I spent some time planning my session, coming up with lots of ideas around explaining my heritage and discussing the challenges of growing up half-Indian in Ireland. But as I sat waiting to be called up, I remembered something one of our leaders had said about taking the opportunity to do things differently – to fully embrace the process of Escape and really break our old habits – so as I stood up to take my place on the stage, I decided I wouldn't go with my plan after all, that I would go with the flow and see where it took me...

I stood up, and announced to everyone what I had literally just decided to do, and pointedly put my folded notes back down on the desk to embrace my free fall, to the supportive sound of encouraging applause from the room. Wow. It was terrifying. All eyes were on me, and I was rambling, very nervously. I was telling them how I usually really like to plan things because otherwise I get very anxious, and being up there on stage without a plan was making me feel very anxious indeed. But eventually I managed to talk my way around to ToGetHer Further, and how I was really passionate about helping women who were unhappy at work. And then I shared the story of how I had created a Facebook group to foster a support network style community for ToGetHer Further.

I'd been inspired by Paola's NOI Club, and realised that I could use a Facebook group to create a safe space for women to share and support each other, but I wanted it to be secret, so it would be fully confidential and therefore completely safe for women to share openly without judgement. However, keeping it secret meant that very few women had been able to find it so far. Then, just recently, I'd added my youngest sister to the group, but she had gone and invited all her friends, which seemed to ruin my plans for what I wanted to achieve.

And then, I'd added some other women close to me who had done the same thing! All these women, being annoyingly supportive, ruining my precious plans! Finally, I realised, that maybe I was the one who was ruining things by holding on so tightly to these secretive plans… I decided to loosen the reins a little, and tell a few of my friends about the group, including my new friend, Katie Shore, who was so immediately supportive that I felt as if I'd hired a cheerleader. She was amazing. She became an immediate champion of ToGetHer Further – helping me to believe in myself even when I had no idea what I was doing.

I shared this story of how tightly I'd held onto my plans, and how I'd only really managed to embrace what I was doing fully when I'd been able to let them go, which seemed to bring me right back to that moment I was standing there on that stage. I'd let go of my plans and embraced this opportunity to be my whole, authentic self, and it was exhilarating on so many levels. I felt seen, and understood, and safely held, as well as relieved that I wasn't going to have to do that again.

I learned so much over my 12 weeks at Escape, but the biggest lessons I took away were around facing my fears, and being more visible. In the past, I had tried to fit in as much as possible – terrified of standing out for fear I would draw judgement towards me. But once we were introduced to the concept of 'edge challenges', facing every fear seemed manageable, even ones around being seen. The idea is that you find the 'edge' of your comfort zone, and you gently stretch yourself beyond what would normally be comfortable – rather than leaping into the unknown, finding yourself paralysed in the 'panic zone', which sends you scurrying straight back to the safe confines of your comfort zone. Each week, we would play with finding new edges to test to expand our frames of reference. For me, it began with running for a train, taking the risk that I might very publicly miss it. I then began playing with it at work – testing my visibility by being more open about my extracurricular activities.

One Monday afternoon in January, a colleague innocuously asked if I had plans for that evening, and I decided to test myself by saying that I was planning to attend a protest that evening outside Downing Street, to take a stand against President Trump's planned visit to the UK. My colleague's eyes nearly popped out of his head at my unexpected reveal. I'd never mentioned anything about my political opinions before – in fact I'd attended the Women's March just weeks previously but I hadn't dared mention it to my all-male team for fear of drawing attention to myself as a 'feminist'. But now I owned it proudly, albeit with a strong sense of trepidation – I loudly repeated that I was going to a protest that evening, and that I'd been inspired to do this after attending the Women's March, which I'd found be a very inspiring and life-affirming event. My colleagues were stunned into silence briefly, but quickly made sweeping statements about me being into 'that feminist stuff'. I didn't let it bother me though – I was proud of myself for speaking up and owning my truth. I knew it was just the beginning.

Lessons I learned from this experience:

- The power of making small, incremental changes to expand your comfort zone.
- The ability to find small ways to learn and grow every day.
- The importance of letting go of plans and going with the flow.
- The value in allowing myself to be vulnerable in being more visible, and enabling myself to get braver and live a more authentic life in the process.

Reflection questions for you:

- When did you last try something new, just outside your comfort zone?
- When did you last do something truly spontaneous?
- When did you last take steps to be a little more visible in the world?

Useful resources for you:

- Try using a tasks app like Wunderlist (*https://www.wunderlist.com/*) to capture all the small challenges you are apprehensive about undertaking - these are unique to you so take the time to think of anything that brings up those nauseating butterflies within you.
- Watch this Ted Talk by Cleo Wade on How to Change the World (*https://www.ted.com/talks/cleo_wade_want_to_change_the_world_start_by_being_brave_enough_to_care*).

- Find out more about Escape the City programmes and events (*http://www.escapethecity.org/*).

Finding My Way: Out of the darkness, into the light

15 TAKING SMALL STEPS

Now that I was letting people know about the ToGetHer Further Facebook group, my community was really starting to grow and respond, opening itself up to all sorts of possibilities. As part of Escape, we were tasked with creating a 'Lean Start Up', or 'Minimum Viable Product', to test hypotheses on a small scale to see if we enjoyed the reality rather than the fantasy. I initially dove straight into my passion for writing, deciding my 'smallest version of success' would be to write a book. Thankfully I was given a little more guidance and course correction, and decided to explore running an event for ToGetHer Further instead.

I started with the absolute tiniest step – simply posting in the group to ask, hypothetically, if I were to run an event for the members to meet up, would they attend? The answer was encouragingly positive, even though a lot of members are spread across the world, the majority were London-based and keen to meet. And so my challenge was set – to run an event for ToGetHer Further for members to meet in person. I had already been thinking about doing something as a collaboration with NOI Club, but I'd imagined this would be in August or later that year, not so soon. This was one of the great things about Escape – by taking these little steps, one after the other, you would quickly find yourself achieving goals much sooner than you originally anticipated.

Now that I had committed to this challenge, the next step was logistics – finding a venue in Central London (ideally for free), setting a time/date, finding a way to sell tickets (and then selling those tickets), and of course, planning the format in a way that aligned with the ethos and spirit of ToGetHer Further. I felt fairly confident about the format, having attended so many events in the past, I knew what I liked/didn't like about traditional networking events. I had decided the focus of this event was going to be on the audience, rather than bringing in people to talk at them, I wanted to create a space for women to connect on an authentic level, rather than worrying about small talk or swapping business cards.

With the help of lots of great suggestions from NOI Ladies, I managed to secure a large meeting room at WeWork Southbank Central, which they very kindly let me use for free, as they were so supportive of what I was trying to achieve with ToGetHer Further. The date was set for the 18th May, and tickets went on sale just over a month beforehand – but only for members of the ToGetHer Further Facebook group. I wanted it to be a private event for the members to connect with each other, and take their conversations from the virtual world to reality. Of course this made it difficult to promote ticket sales, especially with a password-protected ticket site for extra-secure privacy. Also, while the initial enthusiasm from the group was supportive, not everyone was free for that particular Thursday evening, and there may also have been a certain amount of hesitation about being guinea pigs for the very first attempt.

The format I chose for the event was 'speednetworking' – with the women put in pairs with a list of non-work related questions, to give them the opportunity to really get to know each other. They were given dice to roll to keep the questions random and avoid repetition. Looking back now I am cringing at this plan, because I can see how limited and restrictive it was – yes I wanted them to get to know each other, but for a lot of the women who came, they had already left the corporate world and were doing their own thing, so it would have been wonderful if they'd had the opportunity to speak about their work. Also the dice very quickly became a pressured test for mental arithmetic, rather than a fun icebreaker. They say that if you're not embarrassed by the first version of your business then you launched it too late – well I felt like I had launched early!

That said, the night did go really well – there were 15 of us in total, with a mixture of some of my fellow Escape tribe members enjoying the opportunity to meet up post-Escape, as well as some friends of mine, and a few women from ToGetHer Further who I hadn't yet met in person – so a wonderful mix all round. And although I learned so much, so quickly, and massively improved the format by the time I ran the next event, I'm really proud that I did get out of my comfort zone and run that Inaugural Get Together. As my friend Katie often reminds me, how can you get better at something if you haven't even done it yet?

Lessons I learned from this experience:

- Start small – even smaller than you think. Tiny steps quickly add up.
- Play to my strengths – drawing on past experience and existing support to use for research.
- Get clear on my purpose to make it easier to stay focused.
- Always ask for help – as much as possible.
- Allow myself to learn and grow with each attempt – embrace a growth mindset and let go of perfectionism.

Reflection questions for you:

- What is the absolute smallest step you could take to explore doing something new? It could be anything from a hobby to a new skill to building a business or taking an alternative career path – what one small thing could you do to start exploring it today?
- Why do you want to take this step? Get clear on your purpose.
- Who could help you explore this small step?

Useful resources for you:

- Listen to the Financial Times podcast on Start Up Stories to learn from entrepreneurs who have successfully built their businesses (*https://www.ft.com/start-up-stories*).
- Listen to Stylist Live podcast with Enterprise Nation on How to Start a Business for under £100 (*https://itunes.apple.com/gb/podcast/stylist-live/id1053525206?mt=2*).

- Attend one of Enterprise Nation's Start Up Saturday workshops to learn more about setting up a business (*https://www.enterprisenation.com/events-page/startup-saturday*).
- Attend one of Escape the City's events on finding or creating work you love (*https://www.escapethecity.org*).
- Watch Simon Sinek's Ted Talk on How Great Leaders Inspire Action (*https://www.ted.com/talks/simon_sinek_how_great_leaders_inspire_action*)

Finding My Way: Out of the darkness, into the light

16 BLOSSOMING AT BLOOMS

If you had asked me, on my wind-down from work, if I was planning to join a co-working space in Central London, my answer would have been an emphatic *'Hell no!'* I had gotten to the point where I was loving my personal space and freedom at home – loving having the opportunity to go for a walk to the lake near my house at lunchtime, or to spend the day in my pyjamas if I wished. Walking into a corporate setting now was starting to make my skin itch – I could feel that I no longer belonged, and like a child longing for the summer holidays, I could see that freedom would soon be within my grasp.

So when Lu Li, founder of Blooming Founders, announced she was creating a female-focused business club and co-working space near Old Street, no one was more surprised than I to realise how excited I was at the prospect. I had been to We Work, General Assembly, and Google Campus – standard start up spaces around London, and to me, despite their attempts to be different, they had all felt very corporate in their look and feel. Also, I hadn't realised until Lu said 'female-focused', that when I was in those other spaces, I had felt quite intimidated – the energy was heavily masculine, and it felt like unless I already had a tech start up to bring to the table then I wouldn't be welcome. Whereas what Lu was describing sounded far more inviting – a club for women to work together, to mentor each other and connect with each other, collaborating rather than competing. It also helped that her promotional images and branding were all softer colours – pinks, light greys, greens – rather than the harsh, darker palettes I was familiar with in my own corporate experience.

The timing was also perfect for me – I was finishing work with the completion of my project in August, but I wanted to give myself a couple of months to fully detox from the corporate life before focussing fully on building a business, so Blooms London opening in early October 2017 suited me very nicely indeed.

Signing up for a founding membership was a big investment for me, but again there was something within me that knew this was right – I knew that this would be the right environment for me to not only grow into my new way of living and working, but also the perfect place for me to bring members of ToGetHer Further for events, meetings, or even to meet for coffee one to one. I was so right to trust that voice.

Having finally left the corporate world, and allowed myself the time I needed to decompress, I embraced my creative working life at Blooms feeling as if I had found my second home.

I ran the second ToGetHer Further event at Blooms on the 26th October – taking into account everything I had learned from the first attempt, I completely changed the format to make sure the attendees truly got the most from the time. I made the mistake of calling it a 'meet-up' though, when it was so much more than that. This was typical of me to underplay and undervalue my efforts. In reality, this was more of an interactive workshop, for women to connect and collaborate with each other (which is what I called the third event).

Lessons I learned from this experience:

- The more gradual, incremental changes I make, the more natural the transition feels – I was so ready to leave work when my project ended that it felt like a seamless progression.
- Being in lots of different communities helps me to stay open to exciting new opportunities – even ones I didn't know I would want or need.
- The right environment is worth the investment in order for me to take steps towards the life I want.
- The more I do, the more I learn – with every event I run I increase my understanding of my community and myself, and value my efforts more.

Reflection questions for you:

- What small changes could you make today to bring you closer to the life you want to live?
- How do you connect to new opportunities? Through networks, friends, colleagues, communities, clubs, organisations?
- What kind of environment do you work best in? How could you improve your current working environment? Are there any small changes you could make today?
- When did you last take pride in your accomplishments and value your efforts?

Useful resources for you:

- Find out more about Blooms London at *www.bloomslondon.com*
- Join a community of women if you haven't already: ToGetHer

> Further, NOI Club, Blooming Founders, Lean In, Driven Woman - find your tribe.

17 TO COACH OR NOT TO COACH

Back in December 2016, I had been preparing to start working part-time, and joining the Escape course, but I was worrying about how vague my plans were for ToGetHer Further. I wanted to have something tangible to bring it all together – something that was clearly defined, and a recognisable way to earn an income. I thought about everything I wanted to achieve with ToGetHer Further, and all the ways I wanted to help women help women, and I realised I was essentially talking about Life Coaching. I'd never worked with a coach before so I didn't know exactly what it entailed, or even what kind of qualifications I'd need, but I loved the idea of having a clear title – becoming a Life Coach seemed a lot less daunting than "quitting my job to figure out what I want ToGetHer Further to be because a voice deep down inside me knows this is the right thing for me to do". It's also a lot easier and quicker to explain to people.

I began by googling my options, of course, but there were so many coaching courses available that I was immediately overwhelmed. Knowing that there were a lot of coaches in NOI Club, I asked them for help, and they responded in full force – so many women offered to speak to me and share their experience and wisdom. It was wonderful. I got so many personal recommendations for the different options available – from The Coaching Academy to Barefoot to Animas – there were lots of short training courses provided across London, often with free taster sessions for you to gauge whether it was right for you or not.

Somewhere along the way I stumbled upon the Post Grad Cert in Coaching at Birkbeck, University of London. Rather than the other private courses, which were run over a few long weekends and then individual study and practice was carried out alone; this was a full academic year, meeting weekly in a group from October to June. This really appealed to me, especially as I knew it takes me a while to truly absorb what I'm doing and to fully own my worth and experience. I knew that it was highly likely it would take me the full academic year to accept what I had learned and embrace my new potential.

I liked the idea of going back to university, rather than paying for a private course – naturally I liked the prestige and security of a university-based course, but I also liked the imagery of returning to school. It felt like an important developmental stage – leaving my job, taking a summer holiday, and going back to a safe space of learning for the year.

It also helped that the Birkbeck course cost almost half what some of the private courses cost. Oh, and you could pay for Birkbeck in monthly instalments over the academic year, interest-free. But it was still a lot of money to invest, especially when I wouldn't be working, and I hadn't originally factored it into my budget when I was planning my exit strategy, so I didn't commit immediately.

As the weeks passed and the reality of leaving work began to set in, I was looking ahead to the near future and how it would feel to be completely free. Perhaps, too free? I liked the idea of having some structure – something to stabilise what I was doing, something to ground me.

I was struggling to tell people that I was quitting my job to "turn ToGetHer Further into a business", especially when I didn't exactly know what that meant. I had built up a good buffer over the months, so I knew I would have enough savings to give me almost a year of time to experiment and build my new business, but part of me was afraid that that year would quickly come to an end and I might be left with nothing to show for it.

I wondered if signing up to the Birkbeck course could serve two purposes – one in giving me a new sense of structure or routine to work around, and two, giving me something tangible to show for my efforts at the end of the year. So even if I did end up failing to build a business, and came back to the corporate world with my tail between my legs, at least I'd have a new university qualification to add to my CV and make up for my time away from the working world. There was also a potential third purpose – I might find I enjoy it, and even if I didn't build ToGetHer Further into a business, I might want to coach people on a one to one basis, which might save me from having to go back to the corporate world after all. Hurrah!

Again I started looking into the application process, but still I didn't commit.

Then, as I scrolled Twitter one Friday in July 2017, I saw a tweet from Birkbeck advertising the course, and it felt like a strong nudge to look into it some more. I decided I wanted some personal feedback or a recommendation before I fully took the plunge, so I shared the tweet and asked if anyone had done this particular course and had any thoughts to share with me. I didn't expect to be contacted almost immediately by the official Birkbeck Twitter account, or to be offered the opportunity to be put in touch with past students, or even the course leader himself. I immediately felt out of my comfort zone, but I drew on the guidance we were given in Escape to 'hustle' our way into opportunities and to say Yes when we can. So I did. Very quickly I received an email from someone in Birkbeck, copying in the course leader, encouraging me to ask him any questions I may have about the qualification. Again, I felt my nerves rising, but I tried to stay calm and decided to challenge myself to ask him if we could meet for a coffee in a week's time to discuss the course in person. I wanted to use my intuition to gauge him and see if the course still felt right for me. He replied very quickly telling me he was about to go on his summer break, but that if I could come in to meet him on Monday, he could spare some time to talk to me. Another rush of anxious nerves, but I said Yes, and made plans to meet.

For most people, that interaction might have been very simple or straightforward – not for me. I was terrified of putting myself out there, afraid of being visible, afraid of being seen in any way. Simply asking about the course, or asking for anything made me feel vulnerable. As if I was putting myself at risk of rejection. But by avoiding those risks we avoid any potential rewards too, and there are so many rewards waiting for us, whenever we are finally ready to take them.

I met with Andreas that Monday, trying to stem my own anxiety, reminding myself that he should be wanting to impress me, just as much as I wanted to impress him. I needed to be calm if I was to listen to my intuition. I'd learned over the years that the quickest way to silence my intuition was by drowning it out with a lot of anxious white noise. So I even made sure to have time to do some yogic Balanced Breathing to make sure I was fully in my body and grounded for our discussion.

As usual, I needn't have worried so much – although my anxious nerves quite quickly turned into excited nerves. The more Andreas explained the course and his thinking behind its format, the more excited I became. Suddenly this wasn't about whether it was a good academic or professional qualification, rather this was becoming an exciting opportunity for me to explore my own relationship with anxiety, to understand my drivers for helping people, to hold up a mirror to myself and see the blind spots I'd managed to miss so far. All the while being encouraged to critique, and explore, and find new, fresh ways of thinking, as well as getting to do a lot of reading, academic writing, and exploring ways of working as a group. It sounded as if the course had been perfectly designed for me. Another one of those clear signs that I was allowing myself to go with the flow, following my instincts, and getting out of my own way.

I was even fortunate enough to meet a former student who had now become a teaching assistant on the course, Raul, when Andreas introduced me to him briefly after our meeting. This simply added to my confidence in the course, getting to speak directly to a graduate who had gone on to make coaching his profession, working with The School of Life.

After I had made the plan to meet Andreas, I had shared my excitement and learning with ToGetHer Further, and in doing so I had connected with a member of my group who had also recently graduated from this Birkbeck course, and was now working as a coach helping women build businesses. So I went from meeting Andreas, to Raul, to going to meet Ruth, but before I'd even met her I already knew I was going to do the course. I was excited about finally starting the application process. I knew I would have to reassess my finances, and tighten my budget, yet again, but that this would be such an important investment that it was definitely going to be worth it.

Finding My Way: Out of the darkness, into the light

Lessons I learned from this experience:

- Always start with Google.
- Then, ask for help from any communities you think will be able to guide you.
- Get personal feedback/recommendations where possible.
- Say yes when opportunities arise.
- Ask to meet in person - people are more willing to help than you realise, and you never know how helpful having a coffee with someone might turn out to be.

Reflection questions for you:

- Is there another way to look at something you want to do? Another option for training or getting experience or learning more about it?
- Is there anyone you could ask for guidance to help you?
- Who could you reach out to today to try to meet and learn from them?

Useful resources for you:

- Try harnessing the power of social media to explore your curiosities - there are many ways to follow your passions and listen to your intuition without leaving your home.

18 LETTING GO

You don't know where things are going to lead you – you can't plan everything, all you can do is keep taking small steps in what feels like the right direction, and trust yourself to do what's right for you. It starts with you. You have to know who you are. You have to be able to listen to yourself, to trust yourself. Once you feel that sense of being solid, then you can start to take those tentative steps. You may feel like you're crawling, you may crave that movie montage where you get to speed everything up and you're sprinting in seconds, but this is real life, where progress is slow, and painful, but it lasts a lot longer.

I didn't know that after I finished Escape I would end up going to a women's networking event in Surrey with Sharon, one of my fellow Tribers, almost six months' later. It was the launch of The Women's Chapter in Surrey, branching out of London, and it was held at the Harbour Hotel in Guildford, just over 30 minutes drive from my home. I had signed up for the event because I'd seen that best-selling author Adele Parks was going to be speaking, and that resonated with me more strongly than seeing any female founders or leaders just then. I didn't know that I would get to speak to Adele afterwards, and share my love of writing with her as she signed some books I bought from her. I didn't know that I would overhear the tall, glamorous, confident woman beside me inviting Adele to participate in her podcast, and feel myself compelled to connect with this woman further, or that we would bond over our mutual interest and connection to Carrie Green's book, She Means Business.

I didn't know that all of these things would happen, but they did, and this is how I met Helena Murphy, founder of The Guide to Growth, who went on to become my coach to help me build my business, and invited me to write this book in the process.

You don't know where life is leading you, but if you trust it, and trust yourself, it will bring you somewhere magical, this I know for sure.

Lessons I learned from this experience:

- Believe, trust, and go with the flow.

Reflection questions for you:

- Looking back, has any small step ever lead you somewhere unexpected?
- What small step could you take today that might help change your path?

Useful resources for you:

- Read Oprah's What I Know For Sure.

Finding My Way: Out of the darkness, into the light

19 DARKEST BEFORE THE DAWN

I finally thought I had a solid idea for ToGetHer Further – something I could test and develop, and maybe even progress into a viable business. I mapped out the idea as best I could, and talked to some close friends and connections to gauge whether I was onto something. Then, feeling more confident, I arranged a workshop with women I knew might either be interested in getting involved, or would challenge me lovingly if they knew I was off base.

I sat in front of these women feeling far more nervous than I'd anticipated – I'd thought I was clear on this idea, that it was a strong one, the strongest I'd had so far. I was determined to build a business for myself at last – I did not want to have to go back to the corporate world after my savings ran out, and I didn't want to 'play pretend' at being an entrepreneur any more, I wanted to truly become an actual female founder. I was so proud of everything I'd achieved with ToGetHer Further so far – it had been amazing watching the community grow and evolve over time, and I loved hearing so many stories of women connecting, collaborating, and even gaining clients from being in the group. But as happy as I was for them, I was starting to feel sorry for myself – where was my reward? Where was my return for the investment I had made so far? At least I now finally had this business idea – something solid that would finally pay off after all my efforts.

I stumbled through my explanation of the idea, feeling my resolve weaken with every misstep, suddenly far less sure of how passionate I really was about this initiative, and questioning whether it was indeed as viable as I desperately wanted it to be. Rather than the strategic workshop I'd expected it to be, the meeting turned into a session of sharing and exploration – I always seem to quickly make things deeper and more intense than you'd initially anticipate.

Putting aside the business idea for a moment, my friend Vix challenged me to clarify who exactly it was that I wanted to help. Rather than getting distracted by all the many ways I could do this, she encouraged me to get really clear on who it was I wanted to connect with and support with whatever idea I went forward with, because if I didn't know who I wanted to work with, how could we ever find each other?

Gradually it became clear that, unsurprisingly, my desire was to help women who were going through a journey similar to my own. I wanted to work with women who were suffering in isolated darkness, unhappy in their work, frustrated by the lack of choice or power in their situation, in order to somehow set them free.

It was almost a throwaway comment from Vix that then sparked a passionate response from me – she mentioned her own coach had questioned whether we should be trying to eliminate that darkness, because isn't it that struggle that forces us to confront what's holding us back, and allows us to make the changes necessary for us to live our lives to their fullest? Would we be where we are today if we hadn't gone through that darkness?

Almost in a constant stream I heard these words pouring out from deep within me:

"It's not that I want to eliminate the darkness. It's more that if you know you might be going through that darkness, or you're going through it and you're scared, just let us hold you. Let us create this safe space around you so that you walk through it, do your learning, do your growing, do what you need to do, but know that it's ok to feel the way you do. Know that you're not the only one who feels this way, and know that there is help and support and resources and information there to make all of this so much easier. But you have to do this journey yourself, no one else can do it for you."

I almost felt light-headed after blurting all of that out – it was another one of those moments where I almost wasn't even clear where those words were coming from, but I knew them in my heart to be true.

But when Vix asked me if I wanted to help women to use their skillsets for themselves – to maybe leave the corporate world and do their own thing, just as I had done – I felt an immediate resistance. I was almost paralysed with fear just at the thought. My chest tightened, and my breathing quickened, and as I tried to respond to her to explain how terrifying that prospect sounded to me, the tears came to my eyes. Clearly not a normal meeting. Through the tears, in a safe space held by these wonderful women, I somehow managed to peel back the protective layers around this fear to understand what was really going on for me.

I left the session feeling grateful for the support from these amazing women, but also feeling completely annihilated and back at square one. I'd gone into the meeting hoping to come out with a clear plan of action and instead I'd come out feeling raw and connected to something really deep within myself. I knew this time was worthwhile, that it would be a good investment in terms of truly connecting with myself and my purpose on an authentic level, but bloody hell it was frustrating. I just wanted it to finally be my time. I was so proud of my friends and everything they were achieving, but I wanted to get stuck into my own business, I wanted to build my own success, after working so hard to get where I was.

I had thought I learned how to be visible, how to really put myself out there and own my vulnerability – but it turns out there are many, many layers to us as complex, emotional beings. It seems obvious that I would want to work with women who are on a similar journey to me, it was less obvious to me why that prospect would terrify me, but now I can see that it was so close to home that it felt too real. Firstly, it was as if I was offering up my own journey and the difficult decisions I'd made to bring myself this far for public judgement and critique – I would literally be offering my own path, inviting others to share their opinion. Secondly, I hadn't yet been successful in this journey, not as far as I was concerned. I hadn't turned ToGetHer Further into a business, or created a source of income that would prevent me from having to return to the corporate world. So who was I to offer advice to anyone else on making changes in their own lives?

These fears are completely rational and understandable, but, to paraphrase Elizabeth Gilbert, that doesn't mean I let them drive.

I sat with my fears, listened to what was coming up for me, and then, encouraged by my friend Susan, I sat down and drew a picture.

I began by drawing my darkness – the cold, terrifying sense of isolation and loneliness, remembering how paralysing my anxiety had felt, and then I drew my path towards the light – the realisation that I wasn't alone, that there were other women struggling just like I was, that I had far more power and choice than I had ever realised. And then, how that light had opened up so many paths for me, and created so many beautiful connections – how my life had been so challenging for so long, but had resulted in so much more beauty than I could ever have predicted.

I took this picture to Helena, hoping she would understand and help me make sense of what to do next. And she did.

Helena helped me to peel back the layers (more layers) to see how all of my ideas up until this point had been slightly distanced from myself – either I avoided specifically naming the kind of women I wanted to work with (i.e. similar to me and my journey), or I avoided getting too directly involved in the process (i.e. wanting to delegate to others or to distance myself by offering a community solution rather than stepping in to take the reins myself). I couldn't avoid this any longer – I needed to step up and take my place in the world.

It turns out, I didn't need to make ToGetHer Further into a business after all – what I needed was to get out of my own way, and allow myself to become what I had been so desperately looking to find. To truly own my story, own my journey, and share my learning with the women who need it most.

Which brings us to where I am today: sharing my story in an effort to remember how far I've come, to fully appreciate and value the learning and wisdom I have to offer, in the hopes it resonates with those of you who need it most.

Lessons I learned from this experience:

- How many layers there are?!? Seriously, there is always more opportunity for learning, growth and deeper understanding, when you're ready to peel back that next layer.
- Things get harder before they get easier - you just need to trust the process.
- Surrounding yourself with amazing friends and supporters will help you to create the right environment for greatness.
- We don't know where our paths are taking us - all we can do is keep trying to take small steps in what feels like the right direction, and hope we find our way.

Reflection questions for you:

- Who do you know who could help you with peeling back layers like this?
- Is there anything you're struggling with right now that you might be ready to peel back a layer on? If so, give yourself time and space to explore it further. Perhaps with a trusted friend, or by yourself with a journal.
- What small step could you take today that might help you find your way?

Useful resources for you:

- Read Elizabeth Gilbert's Facebook post on Fear (https://www.facebook.com/GilbertLiz/posts/980409515374497 :0)

- Watch Marie Forleo with Brené Brown on How to Brave the Wilderness (*https://www.youtube.com/watch?v=A9FopgKyAfI*)
- Read Braving the Wilderness by Brené Brown for the courage to stand alone and truly belong.

Finding My Way: Out of the darkness, into the light

FINAL THOUGHTS

My journey has not been straightforward – nor is it yet finished – but I can look back over the last few years and appreciate how much I've learned in order to get me to the far happier place I find myself. I'm proud of the work I've done, of the work I continue to do, and I am finally ready to help other women to face their own darkness, and find their own way towards the light.

Your journey may end up looking completely different, but here are the six stages I've identified I experienced along the way:

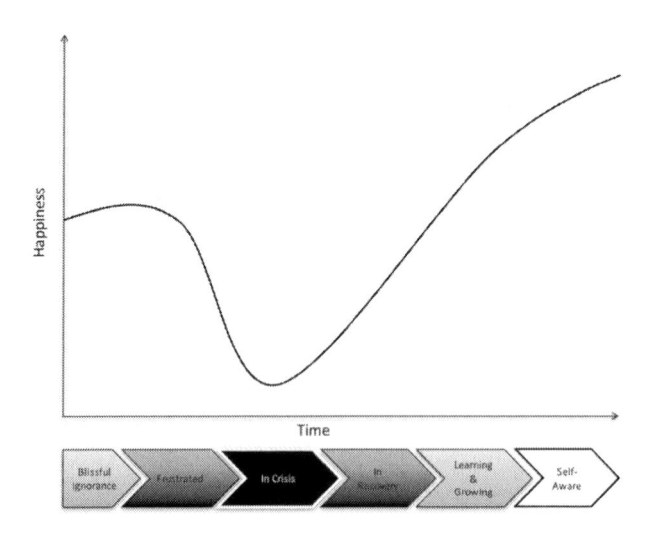

[Graph: Happiness vs Time curve showing a dip and recovery, with stages: Blissful Ignorance → Frustrated → In Crisis → In Recovery → Learning & Growing → Self-Aware]

1. Blissful Ignorance

Before I faced my darkness, I was blissfully ignorant – focused on *"leaning in"* and getting ahead. I had no idea how cut off I was from so much of myself. I had completely bought into conventional definitions of success and had never stopped to reflect on whether that felt right for me. I thought I was happy, but I didn't know who I was or what I genuinely wanted.

2. Frustrated

I can now see that the frustration I increasingly experienced at work was a warning sign. Alarm bells going off to signal that something wasn't right, but I silenced them with new roles, or by changing projects and even industries; trying to throw solutions at a problem I wasn't yet ready to face.

3. In Crisis

Then, as this book opened, I found myself in crisis mode, in a pit of pure darkness. Fighting to even put one foot in front of the other. It would be easy to look back and wish that had never happened, to want to avoid the pain and discomfort that comes with such unpleasant experiences. But it is in this darkness that we do our most important learning. No one else can do this for us – only we can save ourselves. Despite my supportive boyfriend, and the privilege of a capable therapist, I had to do the work to find my own way towards the light.

4. In Recovery

There wasn't just one solution to my problems, but knowing I had the power to make a difference was the beginning to my recovery. Creating that stable routine, choosing to make time to simply sit and listen to myself, gave me the safe space I needed to heal, and gave me the solid foundation necessary to begin the process of finding a more meaningful life.

5. Learning & Growing

Every step I took to help myself was rewarded in some way

– whether by hearing inspiring stories, or meeting kindred spirits, or simply a sense of knowing within myself – I could feel I was on the right path, even when I had no idea where it was taking me. As long as I stayed open to listening to myself and trusting myself, I continued to learn and grow as I found my way.

6. Self-Aware

And finally, I have found myself in a place of increased self-awareness – still working on peeling back layers, still finding new areas of learning and growth, still struggling with the challenges of human existence, but from a place that is so solid I no longer need to look outside myself to find whatever I'm looking for. I look within and I trust myself.

It started with me. So it must start with you. You get to choose.

Whenever you're ready, you simply take that first step, and see where your journey takes you.

And, as ever, remember I am with you; you are never alone.

Love,

Siobhán
xxx

RESOURCES

To help you on your journey, here are some resources that you may find useful – most of them have been mentioned throughout the book but there are some little bonus additions here too, listed in no particular order.

Groups/Communities:

- ToGetHer Further *(http://www.togetherfurther.org/)*
- NOI Club *(http://www.noiclub.org/)*
- Blooming Founders *(http://www.bloomingfounders.org/)*
- The Guide to Growth *(http://www.theguidetogrowth.com/)*
- Driven Woman *(https://drivenwoman.co.uk/)*
- Back Yourself Mentoring *(http://www.backyourselfmentoring.com/)*
- Lean In *(https://leanin.org/)*

Newsletters:

- Harriet Minter - Proceed Until Apprehended, for weekly topical opinion pieces, useful guidance, and inspiration *(https://tinyletter.com/HarrietMinter/archive)*.
- Esther Zimmer – Love Letters, for a beautiful message of love and heartfelt wisdom from Esther *(http://estherzimmer.com/contact/)*. You can also follow her Facebook page where she shares her authentic voice *(https://www.facebook.com/esther.m.zimmer/)*.

Self-Care Practices:

- Article by Kate McCombs on Self-Care Strategies *(https://www.continuumcollective.org/blog/2017/3/7/5-self-*

care-strategies-that-arent-fucking-mani-pedis Warning: strong language)
- Yoga With Adriene for free yoga videos via YouTube (*http://yogawithadriene.com/*)
- Headspace the guided Meditation or Mindfulness app (*http://www.headspace.com/*)

Ted Talks:

- Sheryl Sandberg - Why We Have Too Few Women Leaders (*https://www.ted.com/talks/sheryl_sandberg_why_we_have_too_few_women_leaders*)
- Brené Brown – Listening to Shame (*https://www.ted.com/talks/brene_brown_listening_to_shame*) and The Power of Vulnerability (*https://www.ted.com/talks/brene_brown_on_vulnerability*)
- Scott Dinsmore's - How to Find Work You Love (*https://www.ted.com/talks/scott_dinsmore_how_to_find_work_you_love*)
- Liz Gilbert - Your Elusive Creative Genius (*https://www.ted.com/talks/elizabeth_gilbert_on_genius*)and Success, Failure and the Drive to Keep Creating (*https://www.ted.com/talks/elizabeth_gilbert_success_failure_and_the_drive_to_keep_creating*)
- Reshma Saujani - Teach Girls Bravery, Not Perfection (*https://www.ted.com/talks/reshma_saujani_teach_girls_bravery_not_perfection*)
- Harriet Minter – Proceed Until Apprehended (*https://www.youtube.com/watch?v=gGkdvg76oEg*), and What Yoga Taught Me About Business, Bravery & Bras (*https://www.youtube.com/watch?v=_NnTAlk2vdk*)
- Emilie Wapnick - Why Some of Us Don't Have One True Calling (*https://www.ted.com/talks/emilie_wapnick_why_some_of_us_don_t_have_one_true_calling*)

- Amy Purdy - Living Beyond Limits (*https://www.ted.com/talks/amy_purdy_living_beyond_limits*)
- Andy Puddicombe – All It Takes Is 10 Mindful Minutes (*https://www.ted.com/talks/andy_puddicombe_all_it_takes_is_10_mindful_minutes*)
- Adam Grant – Givers & Takers in the Workplace (*https://www.ted.com/talks/adam_grant_are_you_a_giver_or_a_taker*)

Podcasts:

- Badass Women's Hour (*https://itunes.apple.com/gb/podcast/badass-womens-hour/id1124444087?mt=2*)
- Guilty Feminist (*http://guiltyfeminist.com/*)
- Beautiful Writer's Podcast (*http://www.beautifulwriterspodcast.com/*)
- Magic Lessons (*https://www.elizabethgilbert.com/magic-lessons/*)

Books:

- Brené Brown – Daring Greatly, Braving the Wilderness, The Gifts of Imperfection
- Harriet Lerner – The Dance of Connection and The Dance of Anger
- Elizabeth Gilbert – Big Magic
- Sheryl Sandberg – Lean In
- Dawn Foster – Lean Out
- Carol Dweck – Mindset
- Anne Marie Slaughter – Unfinished Business
- Rebecca Holman – Beta: Quiet Girls Can Run The World
- Maureen Murdock – The Heroine's Journey

- Caitlin Moran – How to be a Woman
- Jess Phillips - Everywoman
- 404Ink – Nasty Women

Events:

- Trigger Conversations (*http://www.triggerconversations.co.uk/*)
- Escape the City (*https://www.escapethecity.org*)
- Alternatives (h*ttps://www.alternatives.org.uk/events*)
- Meet Up (*http://www.meetup.com/*)

ACKNOWLEDGEMENTS

Thank you to my incredibly patient and supportive then-boyfriend, now-fiancé, soon-to-be husband, Gareth. I literally would not be where I am today without your love, guidance, understanding, and faith in my abilities. You not only allowed me to change and grow, you encouraged me to do it, and then went on to be proud of everything I have achieved. I love you and I can't wait to marry you.

Thank you to my not-so-baby sister Fiona, for being my catalyst, for holding up that mirror and showing me what I had been unwilling to see until that point. Your kind, brave step to offer me support when I didn't know I needed it showed me the power of vulnerability and the beauty of genuine connection. I love you and am so proud of you and the wise young woman you have become.

Thank you to my sister Aisling, for reading my work and encouraging me to keep writing, and for understanding my learning process even when I was struggling to find a language to articulate it myself. Thank you for getting involved with ToGetHer Further and contributing to making it the wonderful community it has become. I love you, and I appreciate you, and I am so happy I have you in my life.

Thank you to Katie, and all the women in ToGetHer Further, for literally making my dreams into a reality.

Thank you to Paola and the women of NOI Club for showing me how women can work together in such beautiful harmony.

Thank you to Vix, Susan, Jo, Andrea and Kate for coming together and creating that safe space where I could finally connect with and own my truth.

Thank you to Helena for inviting me to write this book, to own my story and share it with the world.

Thank you to Chloe for proofreading and editing my work, giving me confidence in my abilities as a writer, and the encouragement to keep going.

So many people have helped me along my journey that I won't be able to name them all. In fact, remembering how many wonderful connections and friendships I've made along my journey has made writing this book feel like a letter of gratitude to all of you who shared it with me. Whether I have named you in my story or not, please know that you have helped shape my path, and I am eternally grateful for where we have gotten so far.

ABOUT THE AUTHOR

Siobhán Kangataran lives in Surrey with her fiancé Gareth, who continues to be incredibly patient and supportive throughout her on-going journey of personal development and growth. Siobhán originally studied law before becoming a project manager in the construction industry. She left the corporate world in August 2017 to embark on a more creative, entrepreneurial path with her community, ToGetHer Further. She is very happy with her decision.

You can find more of Siobhán's personal writing on *www.siobhankangataran.com*, and you can connect with her through *www.togetherfurther.org*.

Printed in Great Britain
by Amazon